STERI
Test Prep

# LAW ESSENTIALS

# Criminal Law and Criminal Procedure

## *Governing Law*

3rd edition

This publication is designed to provide accurate and authoritative information regarding the subject matter covered. It is distributed with the understanding that the publisher, authors, or editors are not engaged in rendering legal or another professional service. If legal advice or other expert assistance is required, a competent professional's services should be sought.

Sterling Test Prep is not legally liable for mistakes, omissions, or inaccuracies in this publication's content. Sterling Test Prep does not guarantee that the user of this publication will pass the bar exam or achieve a performance level. Individual performance depends on many factors, including but not limited to the level of preparation, aptitude, and individual performance on test day.

3   2   1

ISBN-13: 978-1-9547250-9-6


Sterling Test Prep products are available at quantity discounts.

For more information, contact info@sterling–prep.com.


Sterling Test Prep
6 Liberty Square #11
Boston, MA 02109

©2022 Sterling Test Prep
Published by Sterling Test Prep
Printed in the U.S.A.

**Customer Satisfaction Guarantee**

Your feedback is important because we strive to provide the highest quality prep materials. Email us comments or suggestions.

info@sterling–prep.com

We reply to emails – check your spam folder

**Thank you for choosing our book!**

# STERLING
## Test Prep

Thousands of students use our study aids to prepare for law school exams and to pass the bar!

Passing the bar is essential for admission to practice law and launching your legal career.

This preparation guide describes the principles of substantive law governing the correct answers to exam questions. It was developed by legal professionals and law instructors who possess extensive credentials and have been admitted to practice law in several jurisdictions. The content is clearly presented and systematically organized for targeted preparation.

The performance on individual questions has been correlated with success or failure on the bar. By analyzing previously administered exams, the authors identified these predictive items and assembled the rules of law that govern the answers to questions tested. Learn the essential governing law to make fine-line distinctions among related principles and decide between tough choices on the exam. This knowledge is vital to excel in law school finals and pass the bar exam.

We look forward to being an essential part of your preparation and wish you great success in the legal profession!

211002vgr

## *Law Essentials* series

| | |
|---|---|
| Constitutional Law | Criminal Law and Criminal Procedure |
| Contracts | Business Associations |
| Evidence | Conflict of Laws |
| Real Property | Family Law |
| Torts | Secured Transactions |
| Civil Procedure | Trusts and Estates |

**Visit our Amazon store**

## Comprehensive Glossary of Legal Terms

Over 2,100 essential legal terms defined and explained. An excellent reference source for law students, practitioners and readers seeking an understanding of legal vocabulary and its application.

## Landmark U.S. Supreme Court Cases: Essential Summaries

Learn important constitutional cases that shaped American law. Understand how the evolving needs of society intersect with the U.S. Constitution. Short summaries of seminal Supreme Court cases focused on issues and holdings.

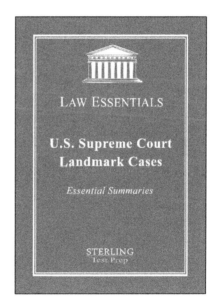

**Visit our Amazon store**

## Table of Contents

**CRIMINAL LAW and CRIMINAL PROCEDURE GOVERNING LAW** (*continued*)

**CRIMINAL LAW and CRIMINAL PROCEDURE GOVERNING LAW** (*continued*)

**EXAM INFORMATION, PREP & TEST-TAKING STRATEGIES** (*continued*)

**EXAM INFORMATION, PREP & TEST-TAKING STRATEGIES** (*continued*)

**APPENDIX** (*continued*)

**APPENDIX** (*continued*)

**Constitutional Amendments XI–XXVII** (*continued*)

# Criminal Law and Criminal Procedure

# Governing Law

Criminal Law and Criminal Procedure are tested about equally. On the MEE, they are usually tested separately. Criminal Procedure may be combined with another topic, such as Evidence. Heavily tested topics include homicide (causation is often tested with homicide), the defense of insanity, Fifth Amendment, Fourteenth and Sixth Amendments, unreasonable searches and seizures.

The statements herein were compiled by analyzing released Criminal Law and Criminal Procedure questions and setting forth the principles of law governing the correct answers. Review these principles before preparing answers to practice Criminal Law and Procedure questions. Memorize this governing law and understand how it applies to the correct answer.

**STERLING**
Test Prep

## Homicide Crimes

For criminal homicide, the prosecution must show that the defendant's act was the proximate cause of the victim's death.

### Murder

When the test uses a word like "murder" or "robbery" and provides no further definition of the crime, it refers to the common law crime.

Know the elements of common law crimes and apply them to specific facts.

If the question wants a definition of a crime different from the common law, they will either define the crime in the question or use a term such as "under modern law."

### Definition of malice for common law murder

The mental state required for common law murder is malice.

*Murder* has four separate definitions.

1) Intent to kill.

2) Intent to do great bodily harm.

3) A death occurring in the course of a felony.

4) Willful and wanton disregard of an unreasonable risk (i.e., depraved heart killing).

A person under a duty to aid another because of a contractual or familial relationship is guilty of involuntary manslaughter if death occurs because of unreasonable failure to give that aid.

An intent to kill constitutes malice (*mens rea* for common law murder).

A defendant must have a mental state of *malice* when acting to end the victim's life to be guilty of murder.

## Murder – intentional killings

*Intent to kill* has two definitions:

> 1) the desire to accomplish a specific result.

> 2) engaging in such actions that the result is inevitable even though not explicitly desired.

The motive behind that intent is irrelevant in establishing intent.

The killing of a terminally ill patient who pleads with a person to end their life is murder at common law because it is an intentional killing.

The consent of the victim is not a defense to intentional killing.

The doctrine of transferred intent makes the killing of an unintended victim an intentional killing if it occurs due to an intent to kill the victim.

If a person employs a mechanical device that kills a person when activated, the intent to set up the device is equivalent to the intent to activate it.

If there are no mitigating circumstances or defenses to the killing, the person setting up the device is guilty of murder.

An intentional killing by a person threatened with death if they do not complete the killing is murder; there is no defense of duress to murder.

## Murder – intent to do great bodily harm

Inflicting severe bodily harm on a victim that was not likely to cause death constitutes murder if the victim dies due to the infliction of that serious bodily harm.

A single blow administered by a fist would not ordinarily give rise to an inference that the actor intended severe bodily harm; a severe and prolonged beating or kicking a victim indicates such intent.

The infliction of a wound with a gun or a knife or other weapon would ordinarily give rise to the inference that intent to do great bodily harm was present.

The victim must die from injuries inflicted with the intent to do serious bodily harm before this malice becomes the malice needed for murder.

## Felony murder

Felony murder occurs only when the defendant is committing or attempting to commit a felony, which qualifies as a felony supporting felony murder.

If the defendant is not guilty of the underlying felony, they are not guilty of felony murder. Often this is the best defense to the charge of felony murder.

A person is not guilty of felony murder if the underlying felony has not commenced or is not completed when the death occurs.

$\underline{M}$ayhem, $\underline{R}$ape, $\underline{B}$urglary, $\underline{A}$rson, $\underline{K}$idnapping, $\underline{E}$scape and $\underline{R}$obbery (acronym MR. BAKER) are common law felonies that support felony murder.

Manslaughter and assault and battery, even though common law felonies, cannot be the underlying felony for felony murder.

Neither intent to kill, nor intent to commit serious bodily harm, is an element of the malice necessary to support felony murder.

An intentional killing during a felony provides two bases of malice for common law murder.

A death that occurs during a conspiracy to commit a MR. BAKER felony constitutes felony murder, imputed to all conspirators when the killing occurs unless the killing was beyond the scope of the conspiracy (e.g., rape by one actor during a bank robbery).

The killing of a co-felon in the course of a felony by a third person does not sustain a felony murder charge against the surviving felon because, under the Redline rule, the killing is justifiable homicide.

## Depraved heart murder

A defendant is guilty of murder if they engage in conduct involving a wanton and willful disregard of unreasonable human risk, resulting in death.

The reckless conduct must involve a substantial degree of risk to human life.

The risk involved is to be assessed considering what the defendant knows, and the risk taken must be unjustifiable under the circumstances.

Examples of conduct that constitute the malice for malignant heart murder (depraved heart murder) if death occurs because of the action are:

- firing bullets in a confined space, through a wall, or into an urban area for confusing police;

- playing Russian roulette;

- deliberately and unjustifiably driving a car onto a crowded sidewalk;

- using deceit to convince an individual to take action likely to get them killed.

## Homicide exam questions

The wording of a question may require discarding the standard pecking order of analysis of homicide crimes.

Typically, felony murder is considered first-degree murder and more serious than murder under the depraved-heart doctrine.

A question may suggest that murder under the depraved-heart doctrine is more serious than killing during a common law felony in a specific situation.

It is crucial to carefully read the question and be prepared to suspend the standard principles of black letter law if the question reads that way.

## Degrees of murder

Since there are no degrees of murder at common law, a question concerning degrees of murder will set forth a statute that controls how degrees of murder are calculated.

Many statutes define first-degree murder as killing with deliberate, premeditated malice aforethought, limiting first-degree murder to planned, intentional killings.

When the malice for murder intends to do great bodily harm or with the recklessness which constitutes depraved heart murder, the murder is usually classified as second-degree murder.

## Voluntary manslaughter

To reduce a murder crime where the malice was either the intent to kill or intent to do great bodily harm, to voluntary manslaughter, there must be:

(a)  adequate provocation to inflame a reasonable person into the heat of passion, and

(b)  the defendant must have been in such a state, and

(c)  the killing must have taken place at a time when the passions of a reasonable person would not have cooled, and those of the defendant did not cool.

Where the malice for murder is felony murder or depraved heart murder, there is no reduction of the murder crime to manslaughter.

A violent battery, witnessing or learning about spousal infidelity, mutual affray, and an illegal arrest satisfy the adequate provocation element of voluntary manslaughter.

Mere words, no matter how insulting, are not adequate provocation for violence.

A second basis for reducing murder to voluntary manslaughter is when the defendant has the right to self-defense or defend another. However, such a defense will not result in an acquittal because it was not properly perfected.

For example, a defendant only had a right to use non-deadly force to defend themself but used deadly force, or a defendant failed to retreat where the retreat doctrine was applicable.

Under the doctrine of *transferred intent*, the killing will be reduced from murder to manslaughter if the defendant killed the victim mistakenly when trying to kill another whose death would have resulted in manslaughter rather than a murder conviction.

### Involuntary manslaughter

Willful, wanton conduct is behavior slightly less egregious than the conduct which forms the basis of malice in depraved heart murder.

A death caused by willful, wanton, but not the defendant's intentional conduct, is involuntary manslaughter.

If death occurs while the defendant is engaged in a misdemeanor, which is morally wrong (a misdemeanor *malum in se*), he/she is guilty of involuntary manslaughter.

Generally, there is no affirmative duty to aid a person in peril and no criminal liability on the person in a position to give aid who fails to provide aid.

A person is under a duty to aid if they have a contractual obligation to do so, their actions (or inactions) put the victim in peril, or there is a parent-child or other family relationship between the defendant and the victim.

In such circumstances, if the failure to render aid results in death, the refusal to give aid can constitute willful, wanton conduct, causing the defendant to be guilty of involuntary manslaughter.

A defendant must act in a willful, wanton manner in performing the act, ending the victim's life to be guilty of involuntary manslaughter.

An unreasonable belief concerning the defendant's threat of harm is not justification for engaging in willful, wanton conduct.

### Elements for murder statutes

Note the terms of the statute given in the question, which separates murder into degrees.

Intentional killings and felony murder are two elements of malice classified as first-degree murder.

Intention to do great bodily harm and depraved heart murder are two elements of malice classified as second-degree murder.

For an intentional killing, determine if the intent was formed due to deliberate premeditation and whether circumstances reduce the crime to voluntary manslaughter or provide a total defense to the murder crime such as self-defense.

## Self-defense

Deadly force is likely to cause death, whether or not death occurs in a particular instance.

Non-deadly force is not likely to cause death, even though death occurred.

A defendant who uses deadly force can successfully raise *self-defense* to a homicide charge if they reasonably believe they are in danger of death or great bodily harm, even if not actually in such danger.

A defendant who uses deadly force can successfully raise a defense if they used that deadly force to apprehend a dangerous felon or to prevent a dangerous felony from being committed

The defense is successful for misdemeanor crimes if the force used is non-deadly.

If a jurisdiction requires a person to retreat before using deadly force in self-defense, a retreat is not required if the person believes that there is no reasonable method of retreat or if attacked in their home.

Even though they are in danger of death or serious bodily harm, a defendant does NOT have the right of self-defense if:

- they are in the commission of a felony,

- a police officer lawfully arrests,

- they were the original aggressor, except when the original aggressor attacks with non-deadly force and is met with deadly force or unless they:

    1) completely terminates their status as an aggressor, and

    2) make that known to the person attacked.

Defense of property does not justify deadly force.

If a person has a valid right of self-defense against A and kills B by mistake, they have a defense to a charge that they murdered B because that killing is justified under the doctrine of *transferred intent.*

## Defense of others

A person using deadly force to defend another, in the belief that the person defended has the right to use deadly force in self-defense, has a valid defense in a criminal prosecution, even if the person defended does not have the right of self-defense because the person defended was the original aggressor.

A person has the right to use the same force, defending others as they do defend themself.

The right to use the same force is not limited to family members.

## Other defenses to homicide crimes

Justifiable homicide is a killing permitted by law, such as the killing by the executioner in a death penalty case or the killing by soldiers on the battlefield.

Justifiable homicide is not criminal homicide.

Duress occurs when an individual commits an act against their will because of a fear of death or substantial bodily harm threatened by another human being.

Necessity relates to coercion by nonhuman elements, such as natural forces threatening an individual's life.

Neither duress nor necessity is a defense to a homicide crime.

In a felony murder case, duress or necessity can be a defense to the underlying felony, thereby eliminating an essential element of felony murder.

*Notes for active learning*

## Other Crimes Against the Person

### Assault and battery

A criminal battery is the unlawful application of force, either by direct contact or indirect physical contact, to a person or recognized extension.

The force may be direct physical touching or using a gun (or another weapon) applied either against the body of the victim or something closely associated with the victim.

Intent or conduct amounting to criminal negligence forms the *mens rea* for battery.

A person has the right to use non-deadly force in self-defense if attacked with non-deadly force.

A defendant using non-deadly instead of deadly force in self-defense against an aggressor does not have to retreat.

The retreat doctrine only applies in limited circumstances to the use of deadly force against the aggressor.

Whether actual or implied, consent is a defense to assault and battery.

### Rape

Consent to intercourse would be a defense to rape even if the defendant committed fraud in inducing the victim to have intercourse.

If the defendant commits fraud in the *factum* instead of fraud in the inducement, the victim does not realize they are having intercourse; their consent is not a valid defense.

Penetration, no matter how slight, is the *actus reus* for rape.

At common law, a husband could not be guilty of raping his spouse.

The underage participant in intercourse cannot be found guilty as a conspirator to commit statutory rape or as an accessory to statutory rape.

In most jurisdictions, the mistake of the underage participant's age is not a defense to statutory rape.

A mistake of age is a defense to the crime of attempted statutory rape.

## Kidnapping

Two elements to simple kidnapping:

>   false imprisonment, and

>   asportation (carrying away).

Demand for a ransom is a necessary element of aggravated kidnapping but not an element of simple kidnapping.

For the false imprisonment element of kidnapping, the perpetrator must confine the victim against their will, and the victim must be aware of the confinement.

Any movement of the victim of false imprisonment without their consent from the place where imprisoned satisfies the asportation element of kidnapping.

## Property Crimes

### Common law theft crimes

The three common law theft crimes are:

> larceny

> embezzlement

> obtaining property by false pretenses.

Since these crimes are mutually exclusive, many questions require distinguishing them.

Larceny requires a trespassory taking; the defendant cannot have the rightful possession when the property is removed from the victim.

Embezzlement is when the defendant had rightful possession when the conversion occurred.

Obtaining property by *false pretenses* occurs when the defendant obtains the property's title and possession due to a fraudulent act.

### Larceny

Larceny is the trespassory taking and asportation (carrying-away) of another's personal property, with the intent to deprive the possessor of the property permanently.

An intent to destroy the property is equivalent to permanently deprive the possessor.

Any movement of the property of another, no matter how slight, satisfies the asportation element of larceny.

The specific intent necessary for larceny (i.e., to permanently deprive the person entitled to possession of the property) is missing if the defendant intended to return the property when they committed the trespassory taking.

If the property is unintentionally destroyed while in possession of a defendant who took it with the intent to return it, the defendant is not guilty of larceny.

If the defendant does not intend to steal because they mistakenly think, either reasonably or unreasonably, that the property belongs to them, they are not guilty of larceny.

The trespassory taking element of larceny is satisfied if an innocent agent takes the property at the defendant's direction.

A person holding title to property can be guilty of larceny if they wrongfully take that property from a person entitled to possession of it.

If a lower-level employee is in physical possession of their employer's property, the employee only has custody of it.

## Embezzlement

Embezzlement is completed when a person in rightful possession of property converts it to their use to permanently deprive the property owner.

Without "possession" of the goods, the crime is larceny, not embezzlement.

An offer to return the property later does not negate the crime.

Embezzlement only occurs when the defendant in rightful possession of the personal property of another converts it to their use.

If a defendant converts property to their use and intends to steal, they are guilty of the crime of larceny, not embezzlement.

If a bailee, who has possession of the totality of the goods entrusted to them by the bailor, breaks into the container holding goods and takes a portion, they are deemed only to have custody of the goods taken.

## Obtaining property by false pretenses

To constitute the crime of obtaining property by false pretenses:

1) There must be a false material fact.

2) The defendant must know that it is false; an honest but unreasonable belief that the statement is true is not enough to constitute guilt.

3) The victim must rely on the statement of material fact.

4) The defendant must obtain title to the property. If the property is cash and is deliberately delivered to the defendant, the defendant's possession would equal title.

5) The defendant must intend to deprive the victim of the property permanently.

An honest belief in the truth of the defendant's representation, even if that belief is unreasonable, negates the specific intent necessary for the crime of obtaining property by false pretenses.

## Larceny by trick

Larceny by trick is a form of larceny which occurs when the defendant obtains possession of the property by fraud.

Since the defendant does not have rightful possession of the property when they form the intent to steal, there is a trespassory taking, and the crime is known as larceny by trick.

Even though the defendant has physical possession of the property, this is not a conversion from one in possession, so the crime is not embezzlement.

## Receiving stolen goods

A belief, either reasonable or unreasonable that the goods possessed by the defendant were not stolen is a defense to the crime of receiving stolen goods.

The property must have the characteristic of being "stolen goods" when the defendant possesses them for a conviction to occur.

If goods, once stolen, are recovered by the police, restored to their rightful owners, and offered to a defendant, the defendant cannot be convicted of receiving stolen goods.

## Robbery

The underlying crimes of larceny or attempted larceny are essential elements of the crimes of robbery and attempted robbery.

For the crime to be robbery and not larceny, the trespassory taking must occur from the person through force or intimidation.

The element "from the person" means property within the person's control.

The force and intimidation must coincide with the larceny.

If all elements of robbery are present, the underlying crime of larceny and (if present) the underlying crimes of assault and battery merge into the crime of robbery.

If the defendant has stolen property, the use of force or intimidation to retain possession of it does not constitute the crime of robbery.

The threat to use force in the future and obtaining property through the use of that threat is the crime of extortion, not robbery.

The victim must be intimidated for the crime to be robbery.

## Burglary

Common law burglary is defined as breaking and entering the *dwelling of another* (burglary cannot be committed in your own house) in the *nighttime* to *commit a felony therein*.

Modern statutes redefined burglary to eliminate the nighttime requirement and include all buildings.

The breaking and the entering elements of burglary need not coincide.

To be guilty of burglary, the defendant must have the specific intent to commit a felony on the premises at the moment of the entering. There is no requirement for the intended felony to be successful.

If a person enters through an open door, the breaking element of burglary is not present.

Burglary is committed if the defendant breaks and enters a dwelling house, even if the defendant does not break when they first enter the dwelling.

Breaking and entering need not occur by force.

If the defendant obtains entry to the property through fraud, the breaking and entering elements are present.

Since the common law definition of burglary requires that the property be the dwelling house of another, a person cannot commit burglary by breaking and entering their own home.

There is no breaking when entering through an open window/door or when the premises are open to the public.

A defendant in a space open to the public can be guilty of burglary if they break and enter into an adjoining space not open to the public.

There is no breaking and entering if the defendant opens personal property (e.g., a chest) while the property is open to the public.

A defendant is not guilty of burglary if committing larceny on premises open to the public.

If the original entry to the property was not breaking and entering, the defendant could be guilty of burglary if they break into a portion of the real estate once on the premises.

A defendant is not guilty of burglary by entering a commercial establishment while open to the public, hiding until after closing time, stealing, and breaking out of the property.

## Arson

At common law, arson is the intentional burning of the dwelling house of another.

The definition has statutorily been expanded to the burning of a building, including one's own dwelling house, to defraud an insurer.

Arson has been committed if an act was done under circumstances where there was a direct and strong likelihood that a fire would result even if the defendant did not desire it, or if the fire resulted from reckless conduct by the defendant.

Since the common law definition of arson requires that the property involved be the dwelling house of another, a defendant cannot commit common law arson by burning their house.

Most jurisdictions have enacted statutes to include burning one's home as arson.

For the defendant to be guilty of arson, there must be combustion of a portion of real property.

The burning of personal property alone is insufficient to constitute arson.

Starting a fire accidentally does not constitute the *mens rea* for arson.

However, if the defendant lets an accidental fire continue to burn even though they could have easily put it out, the decision to let it burn is sufficient *mens rea* for arson.

## Forgery

Forgery is the fraudulent making of false writings that have legal significance.

*Notes for active learning*

## Inchoate Crimes

An inchoate (i.e., incomplete) crime is preparing to commit another crime (e.g., attempt).

### Attempts

A person cannot be guilty of the crime of *attempt to commit* a crime unless they intend to commit the crime.

This applies to crimes, including strict liability offenses, where intent to commit the completed crime is not required.

The crime of attempt merges with the substantive crime if the defendant completes the substantive crime.

If the act which the defendant intends to perpetrate is not a crime, they cannot be guilty of attempt at any stage of their action, even if they think their act is a crime and intends to be engaged in criminal conduct.

An attempt requires substantial preparation to commit a substantive crime. Substantial preparation requires proximity to the place and time of the execution of the target crime.

Attempt is likely to be found where the acts required for the crime have been completed.

Attempt is likely to be found where the defendant has progressed so far that they would be unlikely to stop without outside interference.

Factual impossibility is a defense to an attempted crime if and only if the defendant did not know that the commission of the crime was inherently impossible.

### Conspiracy

Conspiracy is defined as an agreement by two or more individuals for an unlawful purpose.

The agreement among conspirators necessary for that combination can be inferred from the parties' actions and need not be expressed.

To be a conspirator, a defendant must intend to agree with other conspirators and intend to accomplish the conspiracy objective.

Conspiracy is a separate crime from the substantive offense; the object of the conspiracy.

The crime of conspiracy does not merge with that substantive offense if the conspiracy accomplishes its objective.

A conspiracy is a completed crime at common law, even if no conspirator has committed an overt act in pursuance of the conspiracy.

The crime is not complete under federal law until an overt act occurs.

At common law, a conspiracy starts at the time of the agreement.

In a jurisdiction in which there must be an overt act to complete the crime of conspiracy, the conspiracy commences when the overt act takes place.

The conspiracy ends when the conspiracy objectives are accomplished or when abandoned.

A person who is a conspirator is guilty not only of the crime of conspiracy but of substantive crimes committed by co-conspirators according to the conspiracy if they are within the scope of the conspiracy and are committed while the conspiracy existed.

To be guilty of conspiracy, the defendant must combine with at least one other who is not necessary to the substantive crime to commit an unlawful or lawful act by unlawful means.

There must be as many conspirators as there are persons needed to commit the substantive offense plus one.

Ordinarily, two or more persons are needed for the crime of conspiracy.

For example, if two persons are needed to commit the substantive crime (e.g., the crime of adultery), there must be three conspirators.

A member of a legislatively protected class (e.g., a minor involved in statutory rape) cannot be counted as a conspirator.

If all possible conspirators other than the defendant are acquitted of conspiracy, the defendant must be acquitted.

A person who has committed the crime of conspiracy is not guilty of the other conspirators' substantive crimes if they *withdraw* from the conspiracy before the substantive crimes are committed.

To *withdraw* from the conspiracy, a conspirator must disaffirm the conspiracy's goals and inform the co-conspirators of the withdrawal.

Withdrawal is not a defense to the conspiracy crime.

If persons combine to perform a lawful act, they are not guilty of conspiracy even if they believe that the act they are to perform is illegal.

The impossibility of accomplishing the purpose of the conspiracy is not a defense to the crime of conspiracy.

A person is guilty of conspiracy only if they intend to join with another to commit a crime.

## Solicitation

The act of asking another person to commit a crime with the intent that the person asked should commit that crime is a sufficient *actus reus* and *mens rea* for the crime of solicitation.

Once a person solicited agrees to commit the crime, there is a conspiracy between the solicitor and the person solicited.

The crime of solicitation is merged into the conspiracy so that the solicitor is no longer guilty of conspiracy.

## Parties to crimes

The person who knows that the principal is committing a crime and intends to help the principal is guilty as an accomplice.

A person, even though they intend to help with the commission of an illegal act, is not guilty as an accessory if the act which they are helping the principal commit is, in fact, not a criminal act.

Presence at the crime scene without assisting or encouraging the principal does not incur accomplice liability.

If a person present at a crime scene encourages the principal to commit the criminal act, they are guilty as an accomplice.

Supplying goods or services which have criminal and non-criminal uses to a person, with the knowledge that they will be used in a crime, can cause the supplier to be guilty of accomplice liability.

Supplying goods that can only be used for criminal purposes without precise knowledge of their intended use can be the basis for accomplice liability if the recipient uses those goods to commit a crime.

An essential element of the crime of accessory after the fact is that the defendant must have aided the felon to hinder the felon's capture or conviction.

*Notes for active learning*

## General Principles

### General intent crimes

There must be a coincidence of the intent to accomplish the *actus reus* with the actual accomplishment of the *actus reus* for a defendant to be guilty of a general intent crime.

Intent for criminal law is when a person desires a result, and that result occurs.

Intent is present even though the person thought the end would be accomplished by different means.

### Specific intent crimes

To be guilty of a specific intent crime, the defendant must have the required specific intent, which is more than an attempt to accomplish the *actus reus* when accomplishing the *actus reus*.

For example, in the specific intent crime of larceny, the defendant must have the intent to deprive the possessor of their property when they engage in the trespassory taking.

The mental state of maliciousness is associated with an intentional act, but it can be present where the defendant acts recklessly.

### Strict liability

If a statute does not include language requiring fault, a court may impose liability without fault (i.e., strict liability) after considering factors, such as:

> legislative history,
>
> severity of the punishment for the crime,
>
> seriousness of harm to the public created by the criminal activity,
>
> defendant's opportunities to be informed of the facts which lead to an offense,
>
> difficulty of proving *mens rea*,
>
> number of violations,
>
> likelihood that prosecution is likely to occur.

No mental state is required for the defendant to be guilty of a strict liability offense.

A defendant is guilty of strict liability if they accomplish the *actus reus*.

A principal can be guilty of a strict liability offense for an act performed by their agent, which is within the scope of authority.

Specifically, forbidding such an agent to perform an illegal act is not a defense.

To be guilty of an attempt to commit a strict liability offense (distinguished from the guilt of the crime itself), the defendant must have the specific intent to commit the offense.

### Mistake of fact and law

Neither a mistake of law nor a mistake of fact, whether reasonable or unreasonable, is a defense to a strict liability offense.

A reasonable mistake of fact is a defense to a general intent crime.

Neither a mistake of law nor an unreasonable mistake of fact is a defense to a general intent crime.

A reasonable and unreasonable mistake of fact and a mistake of law that prevent the specific intent from being formed are valid defenses to a specific intent crime.

If a crime requires the specific intent of "knowing," and the defendant subjectively does not know that their actions are criminal because they relied on the erroneous advice of a lawyer, the defendant is not guilty of the crime.

### Insanity

If the individual knows what they are doing and knows that it is a crime, delusions caused by mental illness will not establish the defense of insanity under the *M'Naghten* test.

The *M'Naghten* test of insanity does *not* include the irresistible impulse test.

### Intoxication

Generally, voluntary intoxication is not a defense to a crime.

However, if voluntary intoxication prevents the specific intent necessary for a specific intent crime from being formed, the defendant is not guilty of the specific intent crime.

If the crime of first-degree murder requires deliberate premeditation and voluntary intoxication prevents the defendant from premeditating, the defendant would be guilty of second-degree murder.

## Causation

If the defendant sets in motion actions that cause the victim's death, the fact that the victim would have died sooner if they had not set those actions in motion is not a defense to the homicide crime.

A defendant is not guilty of murder, even though they inflict serious bodily harm, which will eventually result in death if the victim dies from an independent cause.

If a defendant inflicts serious bodily harm on the victim, which would not cause death if the victim received proper medical treatment, the defendant is guilty of murder when the victim dies from their injury due to lack of proper medical treatment.

The improper medical treatment is not an independent cause relieving the defendant of liability.

## Justification

A police officer is not criminally liable if they used deadly force to apprehend a person when they reasonably believe that they are committing or escaping from a dangerous felony.

A police officer is not justified in using deadly force to arrest a person for a non-dangerous felony or a misdemeanor.

A person who assists a police officer in apprehending a criminal has the same right to use force as the police officer they are assisting.

*Notes for active learning*

## Constitutional Protections

### Arrest

An arrest warrant is required to validly arrest an individual in their home, except if the arrest occurs while the arresting officer was in *hot pursuit*.

If the person commits a misdemeanor in a police officer's presence, the officer has the right to arrest without a warrant.

A police officer who has a reasonable belief that a person has committed a felony has the right to arrest without a warrant at any place except in the defendant's home.

The fact that the defendant was unlawfully arrested is not a defense to subsequent criminal prosecution for the offense for which they were arrested.

However, evidence seized as the result of an unlawful arrest is inadmissible in court.

### Definition of a search

Only searches by governmental authorities, persons acting as agents, or under their direction and control, are governed by the Fourth and Fourteenth Amendments' exclusionary rule.

The exclusionary rule does not foreclose evidence obtained by searches by private parties.

Searches that require warrants or an exception to the warrant requirements to be valid are closely tied to the concept of a reasonable expectation of privacy.

While a homeowner has a reasonable expectation of privacy from ground-level intrusion in the fenced-in backyard of their home, they have no reasonable expectation of privacy from aerial surveillance.

A homeowner is protected from searches by advanced devices measuring heat escaping from their home.

The person, desk file, and file cabinets in a private office at work, a changing room in a clothing store, and containers of personal effects are protected areas.

An individual does not have a reasonable expectation of privacy in open fields beyond the home's curtilage. Warrantless searches beyond the curtilage of homes are permitted.

The government can obtain financial records in the custody of banks, accountants, or other third parties by a subpoena on the third party without obtaining a search warrant.

There is no search and seizure if the object taken is in plain view from a place where the law enforcement agent has a lawful right to be.

### Search procedure – standing

An individual only has standing to object to searches that violate their reasonable expectation of privacy, not that of third persons.

Ordinarily, the claimant must show a possessory interest in the items seized and a legitimate expectation of privacy in the areas searched.

A search's validity cannot be challenged in a grand jury proceeding.

The proper way to raise the validity of a search is by a pre-trial motion to suppress.

An objection to the admission of improperly seized evidence at trial is available only when the search facts are unknown to the defendant beforehand.

A defendant has the right to establish standing without admitting the seized evidence was under their control and without that admission being admissible at trial.

A guest in a home has standing to challenge a search of that home.

### Search incident to a valid arrest

The police may search a defendant's person and the area in their immediate control incident to a valid arrest.

To protect safety, police may, incident to a lawful arrest, search the premises in which the arrest took place to find other persons who may have been present and involved in the crime.

The search must immediately follow or be contemporaneous with the arrest.

Objects seized in a warrantless search made according to an invalid arrest are inadmissible.

Objects seized in a search before there is a valid ground to make an arrest are inadmissible unless there is another ground than a search incident to an arrest to justify their admissibility.

### Consent searches

Consent must be by either the owner or the person entrusted with the property.

A person other than the defendant can give valid consent to search areas over which they have access jointly with the defendant.

Consent obtained by fraud or duress is invalid.

The consent given by an individual to search their property must be voluntary, but the suspect need not be warned that they do not have to consent.

The superintendent of an apartment house complex or the manager of a hotel does not have the authority to validly consent to the search of an apartment or room in a hotel rented to persons occupying the premises.

## Automobile searches

There is a lesser expectation of privacy in a motor vehicle than in a person's home, and therefore greater latitude to permit warrantless searches.

A non-owner passenger does not have standing to object to the search of an automobile.

If police engage in the random stopping and searching of motor vehicles, the search is invalid.

The police may conduct a valid search of vehicles at a fixed checkpoint, at the border, or the functional equivalent of a border.

If the police have probable cause to stop a motor vehicle, including a stop for a traffic violation, the police may validly search the automobile (including the trunk and containers in the automobile) without a warrant.

The search need not take place immediately. If the motor vehicle is impounded, the police may conduct an inventory search.

## Regulatory search

A regulatory search may be made without a warrant, even if the search is to obtain evidence of criminal activity.

Regulatory searches are confined to businesses and premises that must be licensed to operate legally (e.g., gambling establishments, businesses serving alcoholic beverages) and businesses selling merchandise where criminal activity is likely (e.g., pawn shops).

## Other warrantless searches

A "stop and frisk" pat-down search is constitutionally valid even if there are no grounds for a valid arrest, as long as there is reasonable suspicion of criminal behavior.

The search is limited to a "pat-down" search but may be extended to a more intrusive search if the *pat-down* uncovers an object which reasonably could be a weapon.

A search of school lockers without a warrant is permissible.

## Searches under a search warrant

Police or anther investigatory agencies may not issue a search warrant.

A search warrant may only be issued by a judge or other neutral magistrate based upon probable cause set forth in the warrant application.

The application for a search warrant does not require independent evidence on the basis for the search and the reliability of the informant.

The magistrate can issue a valid warrant based upon the totality of the circumstances.

The application for the search warrant must state, with particularity, the place to be searched and the objects of the search.

If, when executing the warrant, the police find evidence not explicitly mentioned in the warrant, they may validly seize it.

If the application for a search warrant is not sufficient to establish probable cause, but the magistrate nevertheless grants a search warrant, and the police execute it believing in good faith that the search warrant is valid, the property seized according to the search is admissible.

If the police are granted a search warrant based upon information that they know is false, evidence obtained according to that warrant is inadmissible because the search is invalid.

### Fruits of an illegal search

If a search is illegal and information obtained from that illegal search is used to conduct further searches that would otherwise be proper or to obtain admissions from a defendant, which they would otherwise not have obtained, the information or the evidence obtained will be excluded from evidence as *the fruits of an illegal search*.

### Coerced confessions

If either the police or a private individual obtains a confession or admission by coercion (either physical or psychological), the statement made is inadmissible for any purpose.

This rule against admission by coercion applies even if the defendant was given the Miranda warning and waived it.

If a coerced confession is improperly admitted, the conviction will not be overturned on appeal if the admission of the confession constitutes a harmless error.

### Miranda warning

The *Miranda warning* is applicable only when there is interrogation by the police while the defendant is in custody.

An individual is in custody if their freedom to leave the police's presence is restricted.

A statement made to a private individual not working in concert with the police is not subject to Miranda rights limitations.

Volunteered statements are not the products of interrogation.

If the police engage in conduct other than questioning the defendant designed to elicit a statement, that statement is considered the product of interrogation.

Statements made by a defendant in custody due to interrogation are inadmissible at a subsequent trial unless the defendant is informed of Miranda rights and waives them.

If the defendant exercises their Miranda rights by demanding a lawyer, statements made in response to questioning after that demand and before a lawyer is present are inadmissible.

Further questioning can occur only after the defendant consults with their lawyer and agrees to further questions.

A statement given in violation of the defendant's Miranda rights is admissible to impeach their credibility if they take the stand in their trial and testify in a manner inconsistent with the statement previously given.

If the defendant exercises their Miranda right to remain silent while in custody, that silence in the face of accusations made to them that they committed the crime cannot be used in the trial as an adoptive admission.

The police need not inform the defendant of the charge they are investigating to obtain a valid waiver of Miranda rights.

If a defendant waives their Miranda rights and agrees to submit to interrogation, they may be questioned about more subjects than the crime, which is the primary object of the police interrogation.

Once a defendant is indicted or otherwise formally charged with a crime, the right to counsel accrues. The defendant cannot be interrogated by the police except in the presence of counsel, even if given Miranda warnings and waived their Miranda rights.

### Lineups and other forms of identification

A right to counsel at a lineup only after the criminal process (i.e., indictment) has occurred.

The fact of a lineup identification without counsel present after an indictment is not admissible at trial, but the victim can still make an in-court identification.

Testimonies about lineup identification and subsequent in-court identification are inadmissible if the pre-trial identification offends due process standards.

Due process is violated when the likelihood of proper identification is so remote because the victim could not observe the criminal or because the lineup, whether pre-indictment or post-indictment, is very prejudicial.

## Right to counsel

A conviction is invalid if the defendant has not had the opportunity for the assistance of counsel in the trial of felonies and misdemeanors for which the defendant is incarcerated, or the penalty on conviction includes the possibility of incarceration.

A defendant has the right to refuse to have counsel appointed and act as their lawyer.

If they act as their lawyer, they cannot later raise inadequacy of representation or being denied the right to counsel.

A defendant has the right to have counsel provided to prosecute only one appeal.

A defendant's conviction will be reversed even if they had a lawyer if the representation is ruled inadequate.

An attorney representing a defendant who represents a co-defendant may have a conflict of interest, which is so severe that they cannot render effective assistance of counsel.

## Public trial

The public's right to a public trial can be enforced by the news media even if both prosecutor and defendant object.

The court has the discretion to ban or limit the public at a trial if there is a substantial likelihood of prejudice to the defendant or a need to limit access to ensure an orderly proceeding.

## Fair conduct by the prosecutor

A prosecutor has an affirmative obligation to disclose to the defendant material known or in possession of the prosecutor's office, which is exculpatory.

## Speedy trial

The beginning point to measure a defendant's right to a speedy trial is when criminal proceedings commence, not the time that the crime is committed.

The prosecution can wait until the day before the statute of limitations expires to indict and start the clock on the right to a speedy trial.

The passage of time alone does not give the defendant the right to dismissal for lack of a speedy trial.

The defendant must show prejudice from the delay.

## Jury trial

In a criminal case, the defendant is entitled to a jury trial if the greatest possible sentence can exceed six months in jail.

The defendant is entitled to be tried by a jury chosen from a venire in which there is no systematic racial, ethnic, or gender exclusion.

There is a right to challenge the jury's racial makeup, even if the defendant is not a member of the race excluded.

When selecting a petit jury, neither the defendant nor the prosecutor may use peremptory challenges to systematically exclude individuals of one race or gender from the jury.

The state may constitutionally try a defendant before a petit jury, which contains no members of the defendant's minority group if the procedure for selecting the jury venire was proper. There was no systematic exclusion of jurors through the exercise of peremptory challenges.

A judge must take some procedural steps before accepting a guilty plea; otherwise, the plea will not satisfy the process standard that the plea is voluntary and intelligent.

The judge must inform the defendant that they:

> need not plead guilty,

> has a right to a jury trial.

The judge must explain:

1) the elements of the crime with which the defendant is charged, and

2) the maximum possible legal penalty.

## Confrontation

The prosecution has satisfied the defendant's right to confront the witness if the witness appeared at a preliminary hearing where the defendant had the right to cross-examine, and there is a valid excuse for the witness's failure to appear at trial.

Then, the evidence given at the preliminary hearing is admissible under the prior testimony exception to the hearsay rule.

A criminal defendant does not have the Sixth Amendment constitutional right to confront their accuser at a preliminary hearing.

If the accuser is a child who might suffer substantial emotional damage by appearing in the same room as the defendant, the accused's right to confront the witness is satisfied by watching the testimony electronically.

## Severance

When two individuals are charged with the same crime and one has given a confession that implicates the other, the non-confessing defendant has the right to have their trial severed from that of the confessing defendant unless the statements in the confession implicating the non-confessing defendant can be excised.

When a confession is admissible against the confessing defendant but is inadmissible against the non-confessing defendant, severance is not required under *Nelson v. O'Neil* (1971) if the confessing defendant testifies at trial because the non-confessing defendant has the right to cross-examine about the truthfulness of that confession.

## Standard of proof

To satisfy its burden of proof in a criminal case, the prosecution must prove *all elements of the offense beyond a reasonable doubt*.

In a murder case, the burden of proof includes showing that the elements which would reduce murder to manslaughter are not present.

If state law so provides, the defendant can be given the obligation to plead affirmative defenses and prove them by a preponderance of the evidence.

Unless the state has shifted the burden of proof of insanity to the defendant, once a criminal defendant has raised the defense of insanity, the prosecution must prove that the defendant is sane beyond a reasonable doubt.

In a voluntary manslaughter prosecution, lack of justification is an element of the crime and must be proven by the prosecution beyond a reasonable doubt.

## Imposition of the death penalty

A court can only order the death penalty if the defendant has committed murder.

When there is a felony murder where several conspirators participated in the felony, the death penalty can only be administered to the individual who caused the death.

A statute mandating the death penalty for a specific crime is unconstitutional because a jury must have the opportunity to impose the death penalty only after considering mitigating factors.

The death penalty can only be imposed by a jury.

A judge can not impose the death penalty after the jury has convicted the defendant of the substantive crime.

## Fair trial – post-trial stage

The appellate court may constitutionally vacate a sentence and order a new trial if it determines that the verdict is against the weight of the evidence.

While the prosecution cannot, except in rebuttal, introduce a defendant's criminal record in a criminal trial, the judge can review the record for purposes of deciding the appropriate sentence.

## Double jeopardy

Jeopardy attaches to the double jeopardy clause in a criminal jury trial when the jury is sworn.

In a jury-waived trial, the double jeopardy clause becomes operational when the first witness begins to testify.

The defendant does not have the defense of double jeopardy when the judge declares a mistrial to benefit the defendant or appellate court orders a new trial from the defendant's appeal.

The prosecution has the right to appeal a criminal judgment of not guilty only if the appeals court's judgment will have the right to reinstitute a guilty verdict, and there will be no new trial.

If a defendant is tried and convicted of a criminal offense of assault and battery, and the victim later dies, the defense of double jeopardy does not apply to a subsequent homicide prosecution for the death arising out of the acts which constituted the assault and battery.

The statute of limitations on criminal activity starts to run when the last act, an element of the crime, occurs.

Double jeopardy prevents prosecution in a subsequent case for any crime with an essential element of the crime prosecuted earlier.

Double jeopardy does not prevent prosecution for a crime that coincided with but was not an essential element of the crime which was first prosecuted.

## Collateral estoppel

Under the collateral estoppel (issue preclusion) branch of the double jeopardy clause, the prosecution may not constitutionally litigate issues that have been litigated and decided in favor of the defendant in a previous criminal case.

*Notes for active learning*

## Guilty Pleas and Plea Bargaining

### Plea colloquy

The plea conversation between a judge and a criminal defendant has four requirements:

nature of the charge,

maximum authorized sentence and mandatory minimum,

defendant's right to plead not guilty and go to trial, and

by pleading guilty, a defendant is waiving trial, and the case proceeds to sentence.

The court must ask the defendant if they understand each of these points and receive a voluntary affirmative response.

Failure by the court to advise the defendant of any of the above supplies grounds for a collateral attack of the plea.

If such an attack is successful, the guilty plea will be withdrawn, and the defendant will be allowed to enter a new plea.

A defendant may withdraw a guilty plea after sentencing if:

problem with a colloquy,

jurisdictional defect,

defendant prevails if deprived of effective assistance of counsel, and

prosecutor fails to fulfill their agreement.

### Fifth Amendment privilege against compelled testimony

Anyone can assert the privilege in *any* proceeding where an individual testifies under oath.

Must be asserted *at the first opportunity,* or else it is lost.

Privilege against compelled testimony:

protected from compelled testimony only, does not apply to the state's use of a person's biological samples, and

prosecutors cannot comment on the assertion of the privilege.

**Eliminating privilege against compelled testimony**

There are three methods to eliminate the privilege against compelled testimony.

1) Immunity grant for the use and derivative use of testimony. The prosecution cannot use the defendant's testimony, or anything derived from it to convict.

   *However,* a defendant can be convicted based on evidence obtained before a grant of immunity.

2) Defendant takes the stand and waives the Fifth Amendment right against self-incrimination as to anything properly within the scope of cross-examination.

3) The statute of limitations has run on the underlying crime because of no criminal prosecution.

**Punishment**

Eighth Amendment prohibits:

1) Criminal penalties *grossly* disproportionate to the seriousness of the offense.

2) Death penalty statute that creates an automatic category for imposition.

3) Juries must be allowed to hear *all potentially mitigating evidence.*

4) Death penalty *prohibited* for a mentally disabled person, presently insane or was under 18 at the time of the offense.

## Criminal Law and Procedure – Quick Facts

1. **Attempting**, even *with* criminal intent, to do an act that is *not* itself a crime is *not* a conviction that is likely to be upheld.

2. **Larceny** – the **taking** and **asportation** (i.e., carrying away) of another's personal property by *trespass* and with **intent to permanently deprive** the person of their interest in the property.

   For example, the moving of a refrigerator (e.g., by salesclerk) to the loading dock constitutes a taking and carrying away; since the clerk did *not* have permission to move merchandise in this way, it was trespassory. Since the clerk intended to permanently deprive the store of an interest in the refrigerator when they moved it, their subsequent *change of heart* was **too late**.

3. The element of **carrying away** (i.e., **asportation**) is satisfied when there is a **movement** of the property as **a step** in carrying it away.

4. The **continuing trespass doctrine** renders continued possession of the property to be trespassory.

   So, if the trespasser later develops the intent to steal, the actions are considered **larceny**.

5. **Attempted murder** is a *specific intent* crime, though a defendant can be found guilty of murder when their actions demonstrate a very high degree of recklessness.

   If the charge is **attempted murder**, it *must* be shown that the defendant committed an act with the **intent** to kill someone.

6. The Fourth Amendment is *not* violated by a statute authorizing warrantless searches of a **probationer's home** with reasonable grounds to believe contraband is present.

7. If a statute is intended to **protect members of a limited class from exploitation**, members of that class are presumed to be immune from liability, even if they participated in the crime in a manner that would otherwise make them liable.

8. The defendant has a legitimate defense where the **statute** under which charged was ***not published or made reasonably available*** before the conduct.

9. For an **affirmative defense** (e.g., insanity), it is permissible to impose the **burden of proof on the defendant**.

10. **Larceny by trick** occurs when property **possession** is obtained by **misrepresentation**.

11. **Pretenses** are the appropriate offense when the misrepresentations have prompted the victim to **convey title** of the property to the defendant.

Relationship matrix

Topic

*Notes for active learning*

*Notes for active learning*

## Review Questions

### Multiple-choice questions

**1.** A criminal conviction requires a:

**A.** Magnanimous jury vote

**B.** Hung jury vote

**C.** Divided jury vote

**D.** Unanimous jury vote

**2.** A plurality decision means:

**A.** A majority cannot agree as to the outcome of the case

**B.** A agree with the majority outcome, but not with the reasoning

**C.** A tie vote is cast

**D.** None of the above

**3.** The RICO statute was created in response to:

**A.** Corrupt politicians

**B.** Organized crime

**C.** Recidivist criminals

**D.** Illegal immigration

**4.** Battered women's syndrome may prove self-defense in homicide cases where:

**A.** The defendant is especially grieved and remorseful

**B.** The woman accused of killing her husband, with evidence of sustained violence

**C.** The victim was not well-liked or respected in the community

**D.** None of the above

**5.** Criminal laws in the United States are enacted by:

    I. Federal government

    II. State governments

    III. Municipal governments

**A.** I only

**B.** I and II only

**C.** III only

**D.** I, II and III

**6.** When two or more persons agree to commit a crime, that is a:

**A.** Bribe

**B.** Contract

**C.** Plea Bargain

**D.** Conspiracy

**7.** A person charged with a crime in the United States is:

**A.** Presumed guilty

**B.** Presumed innocent until proven guilty

**C.** Presumed not-guilty

**D.** None of the above

**8.** Warrantless Searches are allowed when:

    I. Incident to an arrest

    II. The evidence is in plain view

    III. The evidence is likely to be destroyed

**A.** I only

**B.** I and II only

**C.** I and III only

**D.** I, II and III

**9.** The following may be imposed for a crime:

    I. Imposition of a fine

    II. Imprisonment

    III. Retribution

**A.** I only

**B.** I and II only

**C.** II only

**D.** I, II and III

**10.** The protection against self-incrimination does not apply to:

    I. Body fluids

    II. Corporations

    III. Testimony

**A.** I only

**B.** I and II only

**C.** III only

**D.** I, II and III

**11.** *Actus reus* indicates:

**A.** Guilty mind

**B.** Criminal intent

**C.** Guilty act

**D.** None of the above

**12.** The Eighth Amendment prohibits:

**A.** Electrocution capital punishment

**B.** Sterilization

**C.** Life imprisonment without parole

**D.** Imprisonment in isolation

**13.** *Mens rea* indicates:

    I. Purposeful

    II. Knowingly

    III. Recklessly

**A.** I and II only            **C.** II and III only

**B.** I and III only           **D.** I, II and III

**14.** At the arraignment proceeding, the accused may plead:

    I. Guilty

    II. Not-guilty

    III. *Nolo-contendere*

**A.** I only                **C.** III only

**B.** I and II only           **D.** I, II and III

**15.** Crimes can be classified as:

    I. Felonies

    II. Misdemeanors

    III. Violations

**A.** I only                **C.** I and III only

**B.** I and II only           **D.** I, II and III

## True/false questions

**16.** The United States has one of the most advanced and humane criminal law systems.

    True           False

**17.** In a criminal lawsuit, a private party is usually the plaintiff.

    True           False

**18.** Money laundering uses the proceeds of illegal activities and passing them through a legitimate business.

    True           False

**19.** *Specific intent* is where the accused acted unintentionally.

    True           False

**20.** Bribery is a white-collar crime.

    True              False

**21.** Most modern forms of burglary include threatening the victim with force, in addition to using force on the victim.

    True              False

**22.** The burden of proof is on the defendant to show they are not guilty.

    True              False

**23.** The defendant is formally charged in court at the indictment.

    True              False

**24.** Criminal charges may be brought even though the act was accidental.

    True              False

**25.** Most crimes require *mens rea* and *actus reus*.

    True              False

**26.** *Mala prohibita* crimes are those that are inherently evil.

    True              False

**27.** A penal code is found in a jurisdiction's statutes.

    True              False

**28.** Misdemeanors include crimes that are *mala in se*.

    True              False

**29.** The extortion of private persons is called blackmail.

    True              False

**30.** Misdemeanors are less serious crimes than felonies.

    True              False

**31.** For purposes of the SEC's rules, an insider includes an employee at any company level.

    True              False

          

## Answer keys

| | |
|---|---|
| 1: D | 11: C |
| 2: B | 12: B |
| 3: B | 13: D |
| 4: B | 14: D |
| 5: D | 15: D |
| 6: D | |
| 7: B | |
| 8: D | |
| 9: D | |
| 10: B | |

| | |
|---|---|
| 16: True | 26: False |
| 17: False | 27: True |
| 18: True | 28: False |
| 19: False | 29: True |
| 20: True | 30: True |
| 21: False | 31: True |
| 22: False | |
| 23: False | |
| 24: False | |
| 25: True | |

*Notes for active learning*

# Bar Exam Information, Preparation
## and
## Test-Taking Strategies

STERLING
Test Prep

## Introduction to the Uniform Bar Examination (UBE)

### Structure of the UBE

The Uniform Bar Examination (UBE) includes 1) the Multistate Bar Examination (MBE), 2) Multistate Essay Examination (MEE), and 3) Multistate Performance Test (MPT).

The MBE has 200 multiple-choice questions accounting for 50% of the UBE.

The MEE has six essays worth 30% of the UBE score.

The MPT has two legal tasks (e.g., complaint, client letter) for 20% of the UBE score.

### The Multistate Bar Examination (MBE)

The Multistate Bar Examination consists of 200 four-option multiple-choice questions prepared by the National Conference of Bar Examiners (NCBE).

Of these 200 questions, 175 are scored, and 25 are unscored pretest questions.

Candidates answer 100 questions in the three-hour morning session and the remaining 100 questions in the three-hour afternoon session.

The 175 scored questions are distributed with 25 questions on each of the seven subject areas: Federal Civil Procedure, Constitutional Law, Contracts, Criminal Law and Procedure, Evidence, Real Property, and Torts.

A specified percentage of questions in each subject tests topics in those subjects.

For example, approximately one-third of Evidence questions test hearsay and its exceptions, while approximately one-third of Torts questions test negligence.

### Interpreting the UBE score report

**Overall score.** The National Conference of Bar Examiners (NCBE) states the Uniform Bar Exam (UBE) requires a passing scaled score between 260 to 280. Scores above 280 receive a passing score in every UBE state.

The "percentile" is the number of people that scored lower. If an examinee scored in the 47th percentile, they scored higher than 47% of the examinees (and lower than 53%).

The examinee is first given a "raw score,"; based on the number of correct answers.

The raw score is adjusted by adding points to achieve the "scaled score." The number of points added is determined by a formula that compares the difficulty of the current exam to prior benchmark exams.

The comparative performance of examinees on "control questions" (prior pretest questions) given on previous exams form the basis for determining each exam's difficulty.

**MBE scaled score.** Examinees receive a scaled score and not an MBE "raw" score (i.e., the number of correct answers). MBE scores are scaled scores calculated by the NCBE through a statistical process used for standardized tests.

According to the NCBE, this statistical process adjusts raw scores on the current exam to account for differences in difficulty compared to previously administered exams. The scaled score is calculated from the raw score, but the NCBE does not publish the conversion formula.

Since the MBE is a scaled score, equating makes it impossible to know precisely how many questions must be answered correctly to receive a particular score. Equating allows scores from different exams to be compared since a specific scaled score represents the same level of knowledge among exams.

The MBE is curved, so just because a score is "close" to passing does not mean you are close. For example, a 124 may be in the 31st percentile and a 136 in the 62nd percentile. A 12-point difference in scaled scores equates to a 31-point percentile difference. If you are in the 120s, much preparation is needed to increase your score.

For most states, aim for a scaled score of 135 to "pass" the MBE. If you are unsure what score you need, divide the passing score by two. For example, if a 270 is needed to pass the bar, divide 268 by two to yield 135 as a threshold score on the MBE.

## The importance of the MBE score

A passing MBE score depends on the jurisdiction. In jurisdictions that score on a 200-point scale, the passing score is the overall score. Passing scores are often approximately 135.

For the July 2020 bar exam, the national average MBE score was 146.1, an increase of 5 points from the July 2019 national average of 141.1.

For comparison, on the July 2018 bar, the national average MBE score was 139.5, a decrease of about 2.2 points from the July 2017 national average of 141.7.

How much the MBE contributes depends on the jurisdiction. Each jurisdiction has its policy for the relative weight given to the MBE compared to other bar exam components.

For Uniform Bar Examination (UBE) jurisdictions, the MBE component is 50%.

Most jurisdictions combine the MBE score with the state essay exam score.

The overall state candidates' performance on the MBE controls the raw state essay's conversion to scaled scores. Achieve a scaled MBE score of at least 135 to pass the bar.

## MEE and MPT scores

In a UBE score report, there are six scores for the Multistate Essay Exam (MEE) and two for the Multistate Performance Test (MPT). Most states release this information.

Most states grade on a 1–6 scale (some use another scale).

In states grading on a 1–6 scale, 4 is considered a passing score.

The MEE and MPT sections are not weighted equally.

The MEE essays are worth 60%, while the MPT is 40% of the written score.

Many examinees assume that they passed the MPT and MEE portions of the exam. Examine the score report to see how you performed on these portions.

## The objective of the Multistate Bar Exam

Working knowledge of the MBE objectives, the skills it tests, how it is drafted, the relationship of the parts of an MBE question, and the testing limitations provide you a substantial advantage in choosing the correct answers to MBE questions and passing the bar.

Knowing which issues are tested and the form in which they are tested makes it more manageable to learn the large body of substantive law.

The MBE's fundamental objective is to measure fairly, and efficiently which law school graduates have the necessary academic qualifications to be admitted to the bar and exceed this threshold.

The multiple-choice exam used to accomplish this objective must be of a consistent level of difficulty.

The level at which the pass decision is made must be achievable by most candidates.

The MBE tests the following skills:

- reading carefully and critically
- identifying the legal issue in a set of facts
- knowing the law that governs the legal issues tested
- distinguish between frequently confused closely-related principles
- making reasonable judgments from ambiguous facts
- understanding how limiting words make plausible-sounding choices wrong
- choosing the correct answer by intelligently eliminating incorrect choices

---

*Notes for active learning*

## Preparation Strategies for the Bar Exam

### An effective bar exam study plan

There are a lot of great ideas about how to prepare. Follow through with these ideas and turn them into persistent action for successful preparation.

A detailed and well-planned study schedule has benefits, such as giving you a sense of control and building confidence and proficiency.

Pick a date about 12-14 weeks before the exam (November for the February exam and April for the July exam) and use it as the start of your active study period.

Start a month earlier than many others to have a month to review as final preparation at the end.

Students have found this effective. Use an elongated prep period as a study schedule.

Most examinees prefer at least two weeks before the exam to review the material.

By planning early, you will have more time. You may want three or four final weeks to review subjects, take timed exams, and ensure that you are prepared to take the exam.

A few notes on schedule management:

> Do not *start* memorizing during your initial review period. You should be learning every week from the beginning of your study schedule. This final prep period is for reviewing and taking timed exams.

> If you stretch the study schedule over several months, plan review weeks into your schedule. For example, every four weeks, use a few days to review the governing law and take timed exams. This is a practical and fruitful approach as you will be more likely to retain the information.

Pick specific dates for specific tasks; this makes it more likely you will complete them.

Make sure the tasks are measurable. (e.g., practice two MEE essays).

Be realistic about the tasks, time, energy, and your ability to complete the items listed as tasks in preparation for the exam.

Remember to take some scheduled breaks from studying.

Exercise, sleep and take care of your physical and mental health.

If you are not in the right mental state preparing for the exam, you will likely be ineffective when studying and are less likely to pass the exam.

## Focused studying

Some people are better at multiple-choice questions; others do better with essays.

The multiple-choice portion (MBE at 50%) and the essay portion (MEE at 30% and MPT at 20%) are weighted equally.

Doing poorly in one section means it will be challenging to achieve a passing score.

Identify weaknesses early in the preparation process and focus on them.

If you struggle with multiple-choice questions, dedicate extra time to practicing MBE questions.

If you struggle with writing, focus on completing MEE essays and complete MPT practice materials.

By reviewing your performance on released multiple-choice practice tests, be concerned if you consistently miss questions that are most answered correctly.

If you have problems with questions and perform below 50%, you lack the fundamental knowledge necessary to pass the MBE.

When reviewing your answers to practice questions, it is essential to review all questions and answers, even those you got right.

Make sure you got that correct answer for the right reason.

Reviewing the questions and answers is critical for success on the exam.

Spend time reviewing those basic principles and working deliberately on the straightforward (and easy) questions that supplement learning.

## Advice on using outlines

As a user of this governing law book, several of the following points are moot. They are included, so you can be confident that you are using the proper resources to prep for the bar.

Having a useful governing law study guide (such as this book) is critical.

Without effective resources, it is challenging to understand, learn and apply the governing law to the facts given in the question.

Some students use outlines that make learning difficult.

A few common mistakes about outlines:

- Learning outlines that are too long (e.g., more than 100 pages per subject) or too short (e.g., a seven-page Contracts outline). You will be overwhelmed by information or never learn enough governing law.

- Spending too much time comparing several outlines for the same subject.

  For example, using different Contracts outlines and needlessly comparing them. This confusion results in an undue focus on insignificant discrepancies.

- Outlining every subject. If you are not starting to study early, this consumes too much study time. Do not attempt to outline all subjects. It may be a good idea to outline a select few problematic subjects.

Using a detailed and well-organized governing law outline (e.g., this book) is essential; it saves time, organizes concepts, reduces anxiety, and helps you score well and pass the bar.

### Easy questions make the difference

Limitations on the examiners lead to the first important insight into preparation for the exam – the kind of questions that decide whether you pass.

Performance on specific questions correlates with success or failure on the bar.

By analyzing statistics, questions predicting success or failure have been identified.

In general, the most challenging questions were not particularly good predictors of failure because most people who missed them passed the bar.

However, many of the straightforward questions were excellent predictors of success.

The median raw score ranges from about 60% to 66% correct on the MBE.

The National Conference of Bar Examiners (NCBE) writes, "expert panelists reported that they believed MBE items were generally easy, correctly estimating that about 66% of candidates would select the right answer to a typical item."

Depending on the exam's difficulty, in most states, scoring slightly below the median (miss up to 80 questions) still passes.

The most important questions to determine if you pass are not the exceedingly challenging ones but the easy ones where 90% of the examinees answer correctly.

The easy questions usually test a basic and regularly tested point of substantive law.

The wrong choices (i.e., the distracters) are typically easy to eliminate.

Your first task in preparing for the MBE is to get easy questions correct.

**Study plan based upon statistics**

These statistics show that an excellent performance on either the MBE questions (approximately 67% correct) or the state essays (4s on essays) assures you a passing score.

If you fail the MBE by 9 points or the essays by 5 points, the probability of passing the bar is in the single digits.

Put effort into performing well on the MBE questions for the following reasons.

- The questions are objective, and there are enough questions that are predictable concerning content and structure that it is possible, through reasonable effort, to answer 67% of the questions correctly.

- Studying the MBE first has the added advantage of preparing the necessary substantive law for state essays.

- The essays cover several subjects, the precise topic tested is unpredictable, and the answers are graded subjectively by graders who work quickly.

You had three years of law school practice with essays and less experience with multiple-choice questions.

Master the MBE before spending time preparing for the essays.

**Factors associated with passing the bar**

Based on an analysis of statistics from students' performance, the following factors predict the likelihood of passing the bar:

LSAT score

First-year Grade Point Average (GPA)

LSAT scores are a significant predictor of success on the bar because the LSAT requires similar multiple-choice test-taking skills as the MBE.

The LSAT tests many of the types of legal reasoning tested on the MBE.

A lower LSAT can be overcome by a comprehensive study of the MBE governing law, but these students must work harder.

Most of the subjects tested (e.g., constitutional law, civil procedure, contracts, criminal law, real property, torts) on the MBE are taken in the first year of law school.

First-year GPA measures mastery of subjects, preparedness for exams, and the ability to understand legal principles and apply them to given fact patterns.

The MBE measures the same factors but in a multiple-choice format instead of essays.

## Pass rates based on GPA and LSAT scores

Past statistics indicate that law students with LSAT scores above 155 and a first-year GPA above 3.0 are reasonably assured of passing the bar.

They should study conscientiously and take practice MBEs to perform at the level needed, but they have little cause to panic.

Students with LSAT scores between 150 and 155 and a first-year GPA between 2.5 and 3.0 are in a bit more danger of failing and need to undertake rigorous preparation.

They must achieve a scaled score of 135 and take released practice exams and understand the reasons for incorrect choices. They should prepare for state essays by learning the governing laws in this book.

Students with LSAT scores between 145 and 150 and a first-year GPA between 2.2 and 2.5 have a moderate chance of passing the bar from deliberate efforts.

These students should not rely on ordinary commercial bar reviews and need intense training, particularly on the MBE component of the bar. They must devote 50-60 hours per week for seven weeks to prepare for the bar by learning the format and content of substantive law tested on the MBE. They should take released practice exams under exam conditions and conscientiously study the questions missed.

Students with LSAT scores below 145 and a GPA below 2.2 have had a failure rate of approximately 80%.

They must prep faithfully and conscientiously beyond the advice above and must engage in a rigorous course of study, more than is demanded by a traditional bar review course.

*Notes for active learning*

## Learning and Applying the Substantive Law

### Knowledge of substantive law

The fundamental reason for missing a question is 1) a failure to know the principle of law controlling the answer or 2) failure to understand how that principle is applied.

You must know and apply the governing law to pass the bar. If you do not know the governing law, you will not apply it to answer correctly.

Many students *think* they understand the governing law but do not know the nuances. Do not assume that you understand the governing (i.e., substantive) law. It is prevalent for students not to know the governing law well.

Re-learn the substantive and procedural law taught in first-year courses.

A major mistake is not to memorize the governing law outlined in this book.

The multiple-choice and essay portions test nuances and details of governing law. It is essential to analyze the governing law as it is applied in the context of the question.

On the multiple-choice section, many questions require fine-line distinctions between similar principles of law.

Several multiple-choice answers will *seem* correct, given the limited time to answer. If your knowledge of the governing law is suboptimal, you will not make these subtle distinctions and will have to guess on many questions.

For the essay to be developed, you must know the governing law and apply it to the issues within the call of the question.

If you do not know the governing law, you will not state the correct rule in your essay. You will be unable to apply the correct rule to the fact pattern.

**Where to find the law**

The questions must be related to the subject matter outlined in the bar examiners' (NCBE) materials.

While the NCBE outline is broad and ambiguous, years of experience with the exam delineate the scope of material you must learn.

The governing law covered in this book is foundational to the exam. The governing law statements were compiled by analyzing questions released by the multistate examiners. The analysis revealed a limited number of legal principles repeatedly tested.

Review these principles before taking practice exams and understand how they are applied to obtain the correct answer.

The property questions are probably the most difficult. The fact patterns are usually long and involve many parties in complex transactions.

In preparing for the exam, learn basic property principles and apply them. However, extensive studying into property law's crevices is not necessary to score well on these questions.

Feel confident that you do not have to go beyond the information provided in this book to find the governing law.

**Controlling authority**

The examiners have specified the sources of authority for the correct answers.

In Constitutional Law and Criminal Procedure, it is Supreme Court decisions.

In Criminal Law, it is common law.

In Evidence, the Federal Rules of Evidence controls.

In Torts and Property, it is the generally accepted view of United States law.

The UCC is the controlling authority in sales (Article 2) questions.

The NCBE released questions, and the published answers determine the controlling law through deduction.

### Recent changes in the law

The exam is prepared months before it is given because of logistical requirements. Therefore, the examiners cannot incorporate recent changes in the law into the questions.

Recent changes in the law will not form the basis for correct answers.

If a recent change makes an answer initially designated as the correct answer to be incorrect, the examiners will credit more than one answer.

The recent holding of a Supreme Court case will not be tested for about two years since the decision was published.

### Lesser-known issues and unusual applications

Some of the challenging exam questions are based on obscure principles of law.

Missing the most challenging questions will not cause you to fail the exam if you have a solid understanding of the governing law. You can learn these principles and answer the question correctly, thereby improving your overall performance.

There are instances where the correct answers are different from the usual rules.

For example, hearsay evidence inadmissible at trial is admissible before a judge hearing evidence on a preliminary question of fact (e.g., Federal Rules of Evidence 104(a)).

### Practice applying the governing law

Some students know the governing law but have problems *applying* it to the facts.

The exam is as much about testing skills as it is about testing the governing law.

Therefore, knowledge of the governing law is not enough to pass.

You must practice answering multiple-choice questions and writing well-organized, coherent, and complete essays where you apply the governing law to the given facts.

### Know which governing law is being tested

A typical wrong answer (i.e., distracter) on a question is an answer which is correct under a body of law other than the governing law being tested.

An example is a question governed by Article 2 of the Uniform Commercial Code (UCC), where an offer is irrevocable if:

1) it is in writing,

2) made by a merchant, and

3) states that it is irrevocable.

One of the wrong answers states the correct rule under the common law of contracts, where an offer is revocable unless consideration is paid (i.e., an option) for the promise to keep it open.

### Answers which are always wrong

Some commonly used distracters are always wrong and can be eliminated quickly.

For example, a choice in an evidence question says, "character can only be attacked by reputation evidence." This choice is wrong because both opinion and reputation evidence is admissible under the Federal Rules of Evidence when character attacks are permissible.

## Honing Reading Skills

Reading skills are critical. The basic level is reading to understand the facts, identify the issue and keep the parties distinct. A mistake at this juncture results in answering incorrectly, no matter how much law is known.

### Understanding complex transactions

If the question involves a transaction with many parties, diagram the transaction before analyzing the choices.

The diagram should show the relationship between the parties (e.g., grantor-grantee, assignor-assignee), the transaction date, and the person's relationships in the transaction (e.g., donee, *bona fide* purchaser).

### Impediments to careful reading

Two reasons candidates fail to read carefully are:

1)  hurrying through a question,

2)  fatigue due to a lack of sleep or strain caused by the exam.

A careful test taker maintains a steady, deliberate pace during the exam. Practice in advance and be well-rested on the test day.

### Reading too much into a question

The examiners are committed to designing questions, which are "a fair index of whether the applicant has the ability to practice law." Psychometric experts ensure that they are fair and unbiased.

Even though you must read every word of these carefully drafted questions, do not read the question to find some bizarre interpretation.

The examiners must ask fair questions and not rely on "tricks." Reading too much into a question and looking for a trick lurking behind every fact leads to the wrong answer often.

It is the straightforward questions that determine whether you pass, not the occasional challenging question that tests some arcane principle of law.

Therefore, take questions at face value.

### Read the call of the question first

Before reading the facts, read the call of the question because it indicates the task for selecting the correct answer. This perspective focuses your attention before reading the facts.

The question contains many *words of art*, such as "most likely," "best defense," or "least likely," which govern the correct answer.

The call is often phrased positively; the "best argument" or "most likely result."

Read answers for consistency with the question and eliminate inconsistent choices.

### Negative calls

When the call of the question is negative, asking for the "weakest argument" or asking which of the options is "not" in a specified category, examine each option with the perspective that the choice with those negative characteristics is the correct answer.

After reading and understanding the question stem, read the call of the question again before reading the choices.

Analyze each choice with the requirements specified in the call of the question.

### Read all choices

Never pick an answer until carefully reading all the choices. The objective is to pick the best answer, which cannot be determined until comparing the choices.

Sometimes the difference between the right and wrong answer is that one choice is more detailed or precisely sets forth the applicable law. You do not know that until reading all the answers carefully.

### Broad statements of black letter law may be correct

When reading an answer, do not rule out choices with imprecise statements of the applicable *black letter* law.

If the examiners always included a choice that was precisely on point, the questions would be too easy. Instead, they often disguise the wording used in the correct answer.

For example, the Federal Rules of Evidence contain an elaborate set of relevancy rules that limit the right to introduce evidence of repairs after an accident. If there was a question where the introduction of that evidence was permissible, and no choices specifically cite the exception to the general rule of exclusion, an answer phrased with the general rule of relevancy "Admissible because its probative value outweighs its prejudicial effect," would be the correct answer.

## Multiple-Choice Test-Taking Tactics

### Determine the single correct answer

Increase the odds of picking the correct answer based on technical factors independent of substantive (governing) law knowledge.

The examiners' limitation is that every question must have one demonstrably correct and three demonstrably incorrect answers, limiting how the examiners write the choices.

From the question's construction, this limitation may give clues about the answer.

### Process of elimination

Answering a multiple-choice question is not finding the ideal answer to the question asked but instead picking the best option.

Eliminate choices and evaluate the remaining choice for plausibility.

Eliminate choices that state an incorrect proposition of law or do not relate to the facts.

If you eliminate three options and the remaining one is acceptable, pick it and move on.

### Elimination increases the odds

It takes about 125 correct answers to pass the MBE. An important strategy in reaching that number is intelligently eliminating choices.

If you are sure of the answer to only 50 of the 200 questions on the exam and confidently eliminate two of the four choices on the remaining 150 questions. Guess between the two remaining choices, and the odds predict 75 correct.

Those 75 correct, coupled with 50 questions you were confident of the answer, produce a raw score of 125 on the MBE and a scaled score above the benchmark 135.

Unfortunately, you cannot avoid guessing on questions, but intelligent methods reduce options to only two viable choices.

Sometimes you might not be able to eliminate the wrong answers just because you are sure of the answer to one of the choices. Eliminating with confidence even one choice increases the probability of correctly answering the question.

### Eliminating two wrong answers

Specific questions on the MBE are challenging because of distinguishing between two choices when selecting the best answer.

A typical comment from examinees leaving the exam is, "I could not decide between the last two choices."

The positive side of that problem is eliminating two of the four choices.

### Pick the winning side

The most common choice pattern is the "two-two" pattern – two choices state that the plaintiff prevails, and two that the defendant prevails.

The best approach for this type of question is to rely on your knowledge of the law or instinctive feeling to which conclusion is correct.

In a question with two choices on one side and two on the other side of a court's decision, first, pick a choice on the side you think should prevail.

Distinguish between the explanations following this conclusion and pick the choice that best justifies it.

### Distance between choices on the other side

If the justifications following the conclusion for the side you chose seem indistinguishable, look at the explanations for the choices on the other side.

If the reasons for the choices on the other side are readily distinguishable, and one appears reasonable and the other incorrect, reconsider your initial conclusion.

Remember, the examiner is required to provide a distinguishable reason why one explanation of a general conclusion is correct, and the other is wrong.

That obligation does not exist if the general conclusion itself is incorrect.

Suppose choices (A) and (B) on one side look correct; that is, they are reasonable and consistent with the fact pattern. One of the choices with the opposite conclusion, answer (C), seems incorrect or inconsistent with the facts, and answer (D) with the same general conclusion sounds reasonable. From a strictly technical viewpoint, the best choice is answer (D).

### Questions based upon a common fact pattern

There are several instances where two or more questions are based on the same facts.

Look at the second question's wording to guide the first question's correct answer. When asked to assume an answer to a first question from a fact pattern to answer the second question, the probability is high that the answer to the first question follows that assumption.

For example, if the first question has two choices beginning with "P prevails" and two with "D prevails," and the second question starts with "If P prevails," it is likely one of the "P prevails" choices is correct for the first question. If you picked "D prevails," think carefully before selecting it as the final answer.

### Multiple true/false issues

In addition to true/false questions, the exam sometimes states three propositions in the root of the question and tests characteristics of those propositions in the call of the question.

The choices list various combinations of propositions.

The difference between this type of question and the double true/false question is that only four of the eight possible combinations fit into the options. It is possible to answer correctly even if you are not sure of all propositions' truth or falsity but are sure of one.

### Correctly stated, but the inapplicable principle of law

The task of the examiners is to make the wrong choices look attractive. A creative way to accomplish this is to write a choice that impeccably states a rule of law that is not applicable because of facts in the root of the question.

For example, in a question where a person is an assignee, not a sublessee, one of the choices may correctly state the law for sublessees, but it is inapplicable to the fact pattern.

Therefore, these answer choices with inapplicable law can be confidently eliminated.

## "Because" questions

Conjunctions are commonly used in the answers. It is essential to understand their role in determining whether a choice is correct.

The word "because" connects a conclusion and the reason for that conclusion with the facts in the body of the question.

There are two requirements for a question using "because" to be correct:

1) the conclusion must be correct,

2) the reasoning must logically follow based upon facts in the question, and the statement which follows "because" must be legally correct.

If the "because" choice has the correct result for the wrong reason, it is incorrect.

## "If" questions

The conjunction "if" requires a much narrower focus than "because."

When a choice contains an "if," determine whether the entire statement is true, assuming that the proposition which follows the "if" is true.

There is no requirement that facts in the root of the question support the proposition following "if." There is no requirement for facts in the question to support the proposition that such a construction be reasonable.

## "Because" or "if" need not be exclusive

There is no requirement for the conclusion following "if" or "because" to be exclusive.

For example, if a master could be liable in tort under the doctrine of *respondeat superior* or because the master was *negligent*, a choice using "if" or "because" holding the master liable would be correct if it stated either reason, even though the master might be liable for the other reason.

## Exam tip for "because"

Notice that in an answer that would have been correct, the word "because" limits the facts you could consider to those in the body of the question containing specific facts.

The difference between the effect of "if" and "because" controls the answer.

Identify those limited situations (e.g., where the appropriate standard is strict liability) and distinguish them from those that are satisfactory (e.g., if the standard is negligence).

### "Only if" requires exclusivity

Sometimes the words "only if" are used to distinguish between the two "affirmed" choices to make one wrong.

When an option uses the words "only if," assume that the entire proposition is correct as long as the words following "only if" are true.

The critical difference, where "only if" is used, is that the proposition cannot be true except when the condition is true. If there is another reason for the same result to be reached, the choice is wrong.

### "Unless" questions

The conjunction "unless" has the same function as "only if," except that it precedes a negative exclusive condition instead of a positive exclusive condition.

It is essentially the mirror image of an "only if" choice.

For an option using "unless," reverse and substitute the words "only if" for "unless."

### Limiting words

Choices can be made incorrect with limiting words that require that a proposition be true in all circumstances or under no circumstances.

Examples of limiting words include *all*, *any*, *never*, *always*, *only*, *every*, and *plenary*.

*Notes for active learning*

## Making Correct Judgment Calls

### Applying the law to the facts

Most questions give a fact pattern and ask which choice draws the correct legal conclusion required by the call of the question.

The first skill required is to draw inferences from facts given to place the conduct described in the question in the appropriate legal category.

The second skill is to apply the appropriate legal rule to conduct in that category and choose the option which reaches the appropriate conclusion.

The process of drawing inferences from a fact pattern and placing conduct in an appropriate category often requires judgment.

### Bad judgment equals the wrong answer

To make the questions difficult, the examiners often place the conduct near the border of two different legal classifications.

Decide which side of the demarcation the conduct falls on. Inevitably, reasonable people can differ on these judgments.

If your judgment does not match the examiners, you will likely answer the question incorrectly, no matter how much law you know.

Mitigate this problem by reviewing released questions involving judgment calls where the examiners have published correct answers (i.e., their judgment call).

For example, a death occurring because the parties played Russian roulette is considered *depraved heart murder*, not *involuntary manslaughter*.

### Judgment calls happen

Difficult judgment calls occur several times on the exam, and you are likely to make some close judgment calls incorrectly.

While this adds to the frustrations of multiple-choice tests, it is part of the exam.

By narrowing judgment call questions to two choices and guessing, you will get approximately half of them correct.

You will not fail the exam solely because you were unlucky on judgment calls.

The examiners remove many judgment calls by procedural devices.

85

## The importance of procedure

The question may not ask what a jury should find on the facts.

The answer may be controlled by the procedural context of the criminal prosecution.

For example, it is given that the jury has found the defendant guilty of murder, and the only question on appeal is whether the judge should have granted a motion to dismiss at the end of hearing evidence. This is because a reasonable jury looking at the facts and inferences most favorable to the prosecution should not have found the defendant guilty of murder.

The same procedural issues exist when the question asks if a motion for summary judgment should be allowed or if the court should direct a verdict.

## Exam Tips and Suggestions

### Timing is everything

The time given to complete the exam is usually adequate if you practiced enough questions to improve speed and efficiency to the required level.

As you get closer to the test date, just doing practice questions is not enough.

You need to time your practice. Take previously released exams in two three-hour periods on the same day. Since these practice exams are approximately the same length as the exam, you will know if you have a timing problem.

If you do not practice under timed conditions, you risk exhausting time on the exam before answering all the questions.

Practice your timing under test-like conditions to know if the timing will be an issue. If you cannot complete the practice exam, you will have trouble with the exam.

If time is an issue, adjust your pace and continue practicing.

All questions do not require the same amount of time.

### An approach for when time is not an issue

If you can complete 100 questions in three hours, use this strategy. At the start of the exam, break the allotted time into 15-minute intervals and write them down.

Set an initial pace of 9 questions every fifteen minutes.

Check your progress at each 15-minute interval.

If you completed 18 questions in the first half-hour, 36 in the first hour, 72 in the first two hours, and 90 in the first two and a half hours, you are on target to complete the exam on time. At this pace, you should complete 100 questions in two hours and forty-six minutes.

This leaves 14 minutes to check the answer sheet, revisit troublesome questions, or use the time to go a little slower on the last questions when fatigue impairs acuity

If you find that your careful pace is faster than the budgeted 9 questions every 15 minutes, work at a faster pace, but use the extra time on the more challenging questions or in rechecking your work at the end.

Do *not* change the original answer choice unless you have a specific reason.

It is unwise to leave the exam early.

## An approach for when time is an issue

During practice, continue answering questions to complete the section even after the time for self-paced exams has expired. Note which question you completed within the allocated time. Strive to complete the questions within the allotted time during your final exam prep.

If you learn from taking the practice test that you may not finish the questions in the allotted time on the actual exam, skip those questions with a long fact pattern followed by only one question. Keep your place on the answer sheet by skipping the row.

Return to those questions at the end and complete as many as time permits. Before turning your exam in, guess at the rest to reduce the number of random guesses.

Answer every question, even if you have not read the question, since wrong answers do *not* count against you.

## Difficult questions

If you do not know the answer, do not spend a disproportionate amount of time on it since each question counts the same. Mark it in the test booklet, make a shrewd guess within the budgeted time and come back if time allows.

Do *not* leave questions unanswered. No points are deducted for wrong answers.

## Minimize fatigue to maximize your score

The mental energy required to answer all the multiple-choice questions under stress produces fatigue (even with a lunch break).

Fatigue slows processing questions effectively and impairs reading comprehension. You may process questions more slowly at the end of each session and more quickly at the beginning before fatigue sets in.

Take at least two released exams under timed conditions to know how significantly fatigue affects your performance.

Be sure to arrive at the exam site on time. If necessary, stay at a nearby hotel rather than getting up early and risking a long drive the morning of the exam.

Relax during the lunch break and do not discuss the morning session with others.

You should know enough about your metabolism to eat the correct foods during the exam and reinforce appropriate caffeine levels if appropriate.

**Proofread the answer sheet**

As you decide on each correct answer, circle the corresponding letter in the exam book, and mark the appropriate block on the answer sheet.

The answer sheet is the only document graded by the examiners.

At the pace of 9 questions per 15 minutes, about 14 minutes should remain. Spend that time proofreading the answer sheet. Verify the answers circled to be certain that you marked the appropriate block on the answers.

Ensure that there are no blanks, and no questions have two answers.

Do *not* use this time to change an answer already selected unless you have a particularly good reason to change it.

If you have erased, ensure the erasure is thorough, or the computer may reject the answer because it cannot distinguish between marked answers.

If you have time after proofreading, review the problematic questions, and re-think the answers chosen. However, even after careful thought, hesitate to change an answer.

Do not leave any section of the exam early; use the allotted time wisely.

**Intelligent preparation over a sustained period**

There is no easy way to conquer an exam as challenging and comprehensive as the MBE, except through practice and an investment of time and effort well before the exam.

By diligently preparing, practicing questions, and intelligently assessing why questions were answered incorrectly, your skills for the exam will improve substantially.

Continue to improve those skills by following the advice given herein until reaching a proficiency level enabling you to pass the bar. This proficiency is accurately measured in multiple-choice format questions.

Some students will have to work harder to achieve the required proficiency.

The tools are in this study guide, and any law school graduate can be successful in passing the bar if they invest the required time and effort to be prepared.

*Notes for active learning*

## Essay Preparation Strategies and Essay-Writing Suggestions

### Memorize the law

Do not make the mistake of waiting too long before memorizing the governing law. Start learning the governing law early to be better prepared and pass the exam.

Memorize essential principles and focus on highly tested governing law.

### Focus on the highly tested essay rules

Do not treat all subjects the same when you prepare for the essay portion of the exam.

Some governing law topics are tested more than others. It is crucial to focus on the highly tested topics (e.g., torts, contracts. property, civil procedure).

Know and apply enough governing laws to pass the bar – focus on commonly tested governing laws (e.g., negligence) provided in this book.

### Practice writing essay answers each week

Practicing is crucial to a high score on essays. Practice regularly and avoid procrastination for this essential component of bar prep.

Incorporate practicing essay writing into your exam study schedule. To reduce procrastination, schedule time for writing practice essays each week.

For the MPT, practice by drafting full MPTs. Most examinees procrastinate on preparing for the MPT; there is nothing to memorize.

Do not make the *fatal mistake* of not practicing. The MPT portion is worth 20% of the UBE score.

Know the format and *practice that format to* increase your UBE score. This practice will increase your score and the probability of passing the bar.

### Add one essay-specific subject each week

The Multistate Essay Exam (MEE) subjects include the 7 MBE subjects plus the 5 subjects of Business Associations (Agency, Partnerships, Corporations, and LLCs), Conflict of Laws, Family Law, Trusts and Estates, and Secured Transactions (UCC Article 9).

Combine highly tested subjects (e.g., torts) with less-tested subjects (e.g., secured transactions) and complex topics (e.g., contracts) with easier topics (e.g., business associations).

From preparation, know which subjects you struggle with and require a focused effort to master the essential governing law.

91

### Make it easy for the grader to award points

Your answer to a question will probably be read in less than five minutes by a grader with a checklist to find that you have seen the issues and discussed them intelligently. Writing organized and clear answers makes it easy for the essay grader to award points.

Use headings for each of the major issues.

If the question suggests a structure for the answer because it is divided into parts or because the facts present a series of discrete issues, use the structure of the question, which is probably the structure of the checklist.

Use the IRAC method for the essay questions: state the issue, state the Rule. Apply the rule to the facts and conclude. IRAC seems simple, but following this approach makes it easier for the grader to know that you identified and addressed every issue and applied the law to the facts given.

IRAC results in more points during the exam.

Do not spend time trying to formulate eloquent issue statements. The question often outlines the issues, so an eloquent issue statement is redundant, and issue statements do not earn extra points.

Many examinees spend too much time developing an impressive issue statement and omit other essentials of their analysis (e.g., truncated analysis section).

An issue statement "Torts" or "Is the defendant liable for negligence?" is enough.

Do not waste time arguing both sides. There are no "two sides" for many essays to argue on bar essays because these are not law school essays.

Apply the law to facts and conclude unless asserting each party has good arguments.

### Conclusion for each essay question

Points will be lost unless you conclude for each issue identified in the facts or are asked to address it in the call of the question.

Use caution starting the essay with the conclusion unless confident it is correct.

Many sample answers provided by the National Conference of Bar Examiners start with a definite and strong conclusion. Use caution to start with a conclusion unless confident (e.g., NCBE sample responses) your conclusion is correct.

Starting with a conclusion that is not correct draws attention to an incorrect conclusion at the start, which may influence the grader disproportionality. The grader may lose faith in your answer from the onset, and it is advisable to have a neutral heading rather than a firm conclusion that is wrong.

**Tips for an easy-to-read essay**

Use paragraph breaks between the Issue, Rule, Analysis, and Conclusion. Paragraph break makes it easy for the grader to read and score your essays. Additionally, this approach makes the answer appear longer and more complete.

Emphasize keywords and phrases. Underline key phrases so the grader notices that you addressed the governing law and applied it to the facts given.

After graders score several essays on the same topic, they scan essays for specific phrases that they expect to locate within a complete essay.

**Think before you write**

Read each question carefully to understand the facts and their necessary implications thoroughly and accurately.

After skimming the question, spend time on the focus line at the end of the question. Review the facts with the call of the question in mental focus.

Write a short outline of the issues raised. Outline in your mind the issues; state to yourself the tentative conclusions; test each conclusion from the standpoints of law and common sense; revise, as necessary.

Decide on a logical, orderly, and convincing arrangement for the response. Until then, you are not ready to write the answer.

Of the thirty-six minutes allotted to each essay, spend 15 minutes on issue spotting and organization and about twenty minutes writing the answer.

**The ability to think and communicate like a lawyer**

The Board knows that you have completed law school, under competent instructors, and have passed law school exams. The bar does not challenge the results of your law school courses.

The exam tests the ability to apply what you have learned to facts that might arise in practice and which, in some instances, involve several fields of law. The value of an answer depends not only on the correctness of the conclusions but on displaying essential legal principles and thinking like a lawyer.

Conclude on each issue presented. If a conclusion is derived from fuzzy facts, construct a well-reasoned argument supporting your conclusion to receive full credit regardless of if you conclude the same as the examiners.

If the correct answer depends on a provision of substantive law, which you are not familiar with, you can obtain a passing answer to the question by reaching a well-reasoned conclusion applying general law principles.

Do not try to limit the question to a particular subject area. Many questions combine traditional subjects, and you must be prepared to answer the question applying principles you learned across various subjects.

### Do not restate the facts

The examiners know the facts; there is no time to waste. Do not restate the facts but use them to apply and integrate legal principles in writing the essay.

Do not fight the facts, particularly the focus line of the question.

For example, if the facts state that A executed a valid will, write about valid wills. If the question asks you to argue on behalf of A, do not argue on behalf of B because B has a prevailing argument. However, raise potential arguments which could be made on behalf of B and counter them in arguing on behalf of A.

### Do not state abstract or irrelevant propositions of law

It is usually undesirable to begin an answer with a legal proposition. If the proposition is applicable, it will be more appropriate later to indicate the reason for your conclusion. If it is not applicable, do not state a surplus fact or legal principle.

Although it is seldom necessary to state an applicable rule of law in detail, make a sufficient reference to it so that the examiner appreciates your knowledge of the principle and conditions when it applies.

Do not, by speculating on different facts, nor in other ways, work into your answer some point of law with which you happen to be familiar, but which does not apply to the answer. Importantly, the examiners are not interested in knowing how many rules of law you know, but your ability to apply the applicable rules to the facts.

If the question says that A and B in the above hypothetical are unrelated, do not talk about the results which would occur if they were husband and wife.

Use the principles of law applicable to the call of the question and the facts. You must state the principles of applicable law to demonstrate to the examiner that you know the elements of the rule and how they apply to these facts.

For example, if the facts said that A transferred to B (a non-relative) the money necessary for B to purchase Blackacre from C and asks who owns Blackacre, you would say, "Since A furnished the consideration for the purchase of Blackacre and B took the title to the property in their name, B holds title to Blackacre in a resulting trust for A.

Do not detail the black letter law of resulting trusts since you have shown your knowledge by properly applying the facts to the law of resulting trusts.

Do not fight the facts and address a contrary fact not presented. The examiners may take points away if you make that mistake because you are not focused on the issues presented.

### Discuss all the issues raised

A grasp of all the issues is essential.

For example, if there are three issues in a question, a discussion of only one issue, no matter how masterly, if coupled with omitting the others, could not result in 100% credit. It would probably result in a score of 33%.

The exam includes many issues in most questions so it can be graded mechanically. This maintains consistency across a group of several graders for each exam question.

The grader has a checklist of issues and awards most points for the examinee that identifies issues and intelligently discusses each.

Failure to see and discuss enough issues intelligently is probably the biggest reason for failure on the essay portion of the exam.

### Methods for finding all issues

Use all the facts presented. Failure to discuss facts probably means that you missed important issues.

If you must decide in the early part of the question (e.g., does the court have jurisdiction) and you decide that issue so the remaining facts become irrelevant, make an alternative assumption ("If the court does have jurisdiction") and answer the question in the alternative using facts which would otherwise be irrelevant.

Do not avoid issues because you are not sure of the substantive law. If the examiners stated that X's nephew helped X escape after a crime, discuss the nephew's status as an accessory after the fact. If you do not know whether he is a close enough relative to be exempt under the statute, answer this issue by making alternative assumptions.

### Indicators requiring alternative arguments

*Ambiguous terms* – if there are words in the fact pattern that are neutral or ambiguous such as "put up," the examiners look for possible interpretations of these terms.

*Language in quotes* – language placed in quotes is almost always ambiguous and must be construed as part of the answer.

### Avoid ambiguous, rambling statements and verbosity

Generally, do not use compound sentences. Two separate sentences are preferred.

Complex sentences are particularly useful to apply the facts of the question to the applicable principle of law.

For example, in the previous resulting trust hypothetical, write, "Since B purchased Blackacre and took title in their name with money furnished by A, A holds title to Blackacre in a resulting trust, even if B has not signed a memorandum."

### Avoid undue repetition

If the same principle of law and conclusion apply to two parts of an answer, state it once in detail, and refer back for the second part.

For example, if you have discussed A's liability and now must discuss B's liability, say, "B is also guilty of murder for the same reasons as A. (see discussion above)."

### Avoid slang and colloquialism

The examiners judge your formal writing style.

If the examiner shows humor with names and events, do not show your sense of humor.

Use the standard abbreviations:

P for Plaintiff

D for Defendant

K for Contract

BFP for *Bona Fide* purchaser

### Write legibly and coherently

Printing is usually easier to read than handwriting.

Use all the pages, and do not crowd your answer.

Plan your answer so that you do not have to use inserts and arrows.

## Timing strategies

On the MEE, you must complete six equally weighted essay questions in three hours; an average of 30 minutes per question.

You have flexibility with time limitations as questions are not of the same difficulty.

There are two absolute figures:

spend no more than 45 minutes on any question,

spend at least 20 minutes on each question.

Be careful about not going over the time limit on the first question because this will require a readjustment of your timing for the entire session. If you miss the deadlines, re-divide your remaining time so that you will have an equal amount of time on each question.

If you go over by 15 minutes a question, do not allocate 30 minutes for other questions.

## Stay focused

Do not start by reading the entire exam. Answer the questions in order and do not consider more than one question at a time.

After answering, put it out of your mind and not worry about your response. Keep your mind clear to focus on the next question.

Proofread your answers as time permits.

## Law school essay grading matrix

An "A" answer is an outstanding response. It correctly and fully identifies dispositive issues and sub-issues raised by the question. The answer states the applicable legal rules and sub-rules with precision. It analyzes the question thoroughly with the applicable rules and explores alternative analysis where appropriate. It applies the law to the facts to conclude and is not cluttered by irrelevant matters. An "A" answer demonstrates an objectively superior mastering of the subject. An answer is not an "A" answer simply because it is better than most students' answers.

A "B" answer is a good response. It presents the four components of a good answer (issues, rules, analysis & application, and conclusion), but it does so in a way that could be improved. For example, it may be that not all critical issues have been spotted, or the issues are not presented clearly. The statement of legal rules captures that basic law but may not develop the law's complexities or nuances. The analysis is competent but lacks subtlety and may be somewhat simplistic or conclusory.

A "C" answer is a minimally competent response. It contains the four components of a good answer (issues, rules, analysis & application, and conclusion) but may not distinguish them. Perhaps only some issues have been identified while others are missed. The rules of law lack completeness or accuracy. The analysis and application may be shallow and conclusory. Conclusions may be questionable and not well-defended.

A "D" answer lacks basic components. It may identify the wrong issues or none. Rules are stated incorrectly. The analysis is conclusory or absent. The law is not applied to the facts coherently. Conclusions are unsupported or missing. The response exhibits a lack of knowledge of legal issues and rules or demonstrates an inability to engage in legal analysis.

*Best wishes with your preparation!*

# Appendix

## Overview of American Law

**Overview of American Law**

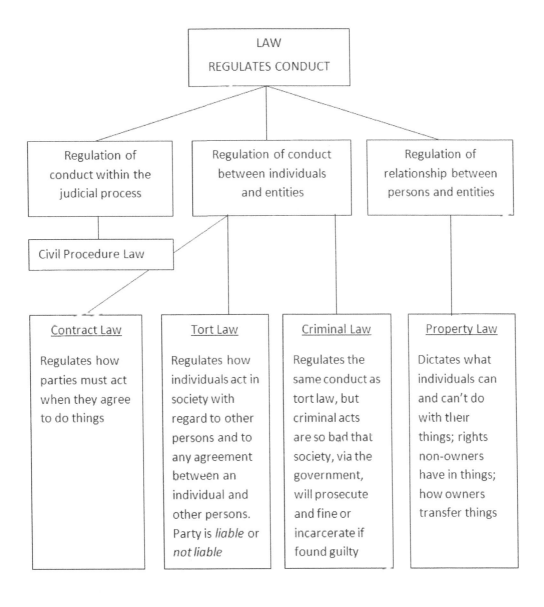

## U.S. Court Systems – Federal and State Courts

There are two kinds of courts in the USA – federal courts and state courts.

Federal courts are established under the U.S. Constitution by Congress to decide disputes involving the Constitution and laws passed by Congress. A state establishes state and local courts (within states, local courts are established by cities, counties, and other municipalities).

### Jurisdiction of federal and state courts

The differences between federal courts and state courts are defined by jurisdiction.[1] Jurisdiction refers to the kinds of cases that a particular court is authorized to hear and adjudicate (i.e., the pronouncement of a legally binding judgment upon the parties to the dispute).

Federal court jurisdiction is limited to the types of cases listed in the Constitution and specifically provided by Congress. For the most part, federal courts only hear:

- cases in which the United States is a party[2];

- cases involving violations of the U.S. Constitution or federal laws (under federal-question jurisdiction[3]);

- cases between citizens of different states if the amount in controversy *exceeds* $75,000 (under diversity jurisdiction[4]); and

- bankruptcy, copyright, patent, and maritime law cases.

State courts, in contrast, have broad jurisdiction, so the cases individual citizens are likely to be involved in (e.g., robberies, traffic violations, contracts, and family disputes) are usually heard and decided in state courts. The only cases state courts are not allowed to hear are lawsuits against the United States and those involving certain specific federal laws: criminal, antitrust, bankruptcy, patent, copyright, and some maritime law cases.

In many cases, both federal and state courts have jurisdiction whereby the plaintiff (i.e., the party initiating the suit) can choose whether to file their claim in state or federal court.

Criminal cases involving federal laws can be tried only in federal court, but most criminal cases involve violations of state law and are tried in state court. Robbery is a crime, but what law makes it is a crime? Except for certain exceptions, state laws, not federal laws, make robbery a crime. There are only a few federal laws about robbery, such as the law that makes it a federal crime to rob a bank whose deposits are insured by a federal agency. Examples of other federal crimes are the transport of illegal drugs into the country or across state lines and using the U.S. mail system to defraud consumers.

Crimes committed on federal property (e.g., national parks or military reservations) are prosecuted in federal court.

Federal courts may hear cases concerning state laws if the issue is whether the state law violates the federal Constitution. Suppose a state law forbids slaughtering animals outside of certain limited areas. A neighborhood association brings a case in state court against a defendant who sacrifices chickens in their backyard. When the court issues an order (i.e., an injunction[5]) forbidding the defendant from further sacrifices, the defendant challenges the state law in federal court as an unconstitutional infringement of religious freedom.

Some conduct is illegal under both federal and state laws. For example, federal laws prohibit employment discrimination, and the states have added additional legal restrictions. A person can file their claim in either federal or state court under federal law or federal and state laws. A case that only involves a state law can be brought only in state court.

Appeals for review of actions by federal administrative agencies are federal civil cases.

For example, if the Environmental Protection Agency, over the objection of area residents, issued a permit to a paper mill to discharge water used in its milling process into the Scenic River, the residents may appeal and have the federal court of appeals review the agency's decision.

---

[1] *jurisdiction* – 1) the legal authority of a court to hear and decide specific types of case; 2) the geographic area over which the court has the authority to decide cases.

[2] *parties* – the plaintiff and the defendant in a lawsuit.

[3] *federal-question jurisdiction* – the federal district courts' authorization to hear and decide cases arising under the Constitution, laws, or treaties of the United States.

[4] *diversity jurisdiction* – the federal district courts' authority to hear and decide civil cases involving plaintiffs and defendants who are citizens of different states (or U.S. citizens and foreign nationals) and meet specific statutory requirements.

[5] *injunction* – a judge's order that a party takes or refrain from taking a particular action. An injunction may be preliminary until the outcome of a case is determined or permanent.

**Organization of the federal courts**

Congress has divided the country into 94 federal judicial districts, with each having a U.S. district court. The U.S. district courts are the federal trial courts -- where federal cases are tried, witnesses testify, and juries serve.

Each district has a U.S. bankruptcy court, which is part of the district court that administers the U.S. bankruptcy laws.

Congress uses state boundaries to help define the districts. Some districts cover an entire state, like Idaho. Other districts cover just part of a state, like the Northern District of California. Congress placed each of the ninety-four districts in one of twelve regional circuits whereby each circuit has a court of appeals. The losing party can petition the court of appeals to review the case to determine if the district judge applied the law correctly.

There is a U.S. Court of Appeals for the Federal Circuit, whose jurisdiction is defined by subject matter rather than geography. It hears appeals from certain courts and agencies, such as the U.S. Court of International Trade, the U.S. Court of Federal Claims, and the U.S. Patent and Trademark Office, and certain types of cases from the district courts (mainly lawsuits claiming that patents have been infringed).

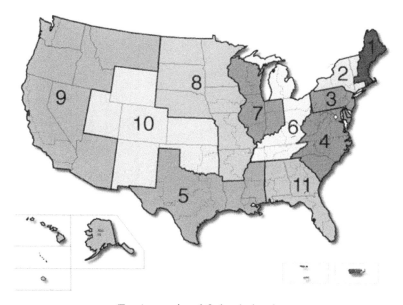

Twelve regional federal circuits

The Supreme Court in Washington, D.C., is the highest court in the nation. The losing party can petition in a case in the court of appeals (or, sometimes, in a state supreme court), can petition the Supreme Court to hear an appeal.

Unlike a court of appeals, the Supreme Court does not have to hear the case. The Supreme Court hears only a small percentage of the cases it is asked to review.

*Notes for active learning*

## How Civil Cases Move Through the Federal Courts

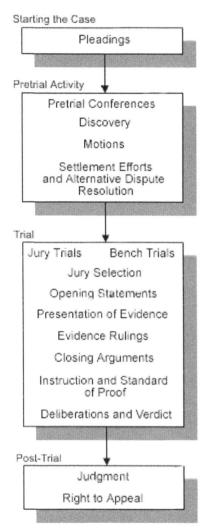

A federal civil case begins when a person, or their legal representative, files a paper with the clerk of the court that asserts another person's wrongful act injured the person. In legal terminology, the plaintiff files a *complaint* against the defendant.

The defendant files an *answer* to the complaint. These written statements of the party's positions are called pleadings. In some circumstances, the defendant may file a *motion* instead of an answer; the motion asks the court to take some action, such as dismiss the case or require the plaintiff to explain more clearly what the lawsuit is about.

### Jury trials

In a jury trial, the jury decides what happened, and to apply the legal standards, the judge tells them to apply to reach a verdict. The plaintiff presents evidence supporting its view of the case, and the defendant presents evidence rebutting the plaintiff's evidence or supporting its view of the case. From these presentations, the jury must decide what happened and applied the law to those facts.

The jury never decides what law applies to the case; that is the role of the judge. For example, in a discrimination case where the plaintiff alleged that their workplace was hostile, the judge tells the jury the legal standard for a hostile environment.

The jury would have to decide whether the plaintiff's description of events was true and whether those events met the legal standard. A trial jury, or petit jury, may consist of six to twelve jurors in a civil case.

## Bench trials

If the parties agree not to have a *jury trial* and leave the fact-finding to the judge, the trial is a *bench trial*. In bench and jury trials, the judge ensures the correct legal standards are followed.

In contrast to a jury trial, the judge decides the facts and renders the verdict in a *bench trial*.

For example, in a discrimination case in which the plaintiff alleged a hostile environment, the judge would determine the legal standard for a hostile environment and decide whether the plaintiff's description of events was true and whether those events met the legal standard.

Some kinds of cases always have bench trials. For example, there is never a jury trial if the plaintiff is seeking an injunction, an order from the judge that the defendant does, or stop doing something, as opposed to monetary damages.

Some statutes provide that a judge must decide the facts in certain types of cases.

## Jury selection

A jury trial begins with the selection of jurors. Citizens are selected for jury service through a process set out in laws passed by Congress and in the federal rules of procedure.

First, citizens are called to court to be available to serve on juries. These citizens are selected at random from sources, in most districts, lists of registered voters, which may be augmented by other sources, such as lists of licensed drivers in the judicial district.

The judge and the lawyers choose who will serve on the jury.

To choose the jurors, the judge and sometimes the lawyers ask prospective jurors questions to determine if they will decide the case fairly, a process known as *voir dire*.

The lawyers may request that the judge excuse jurors they think may not be impartial, such as those who know a party in the case or who have had an experience that might make them favor one side over the other. These requests for rejecting jurors are *challenges for cause*.

The lawyers may request that the judge excuse a certain number of jurors without reason; these requests are *peremptory challenges*.

## Instructions and standard of proof

Following the closing arguments, the judge gives instructions to the jury, explaining the relevant law, how the law applies to the case, and what questions the jury must decide.

How sure do jurors have to be before they reach a verdict? One important instruction the judge gives the jury is the standard of proof they must follow in deciding the case.

The courts, through their decisions, and Congress, through statutes, have established standards by which facts must be proven in criminal and civil cases.

In civil cases, to decide for the plaintiff, the jury must determine by a *preponderance of the evidence* that the defendant failed to perform a legal duty and violated the plaintiff's rights. A preponderance of the evidence means that, based on the evidence, the evidence favors the plaintiff more (even if only slightly) than it favors the defendant.

If the evidence in favor of the plaintiff could be placed on one side of a scale and that in favor of the defendant on the other, the plaintiff would win if the evidence in favor of the plaintiff was heavy enough to tip the scale. If the two sides were even, or if the scale tipped for the defendant, the defendant would win.

### Judgment

In civil cases, if the jury (or judge) decides in favor of the plaintiff, the result usually is that the defendant must pay the plaintiff money or damages. The judge orders the defendant to pay the decided amount. Sometimes the defendant is ordered to take some specific action that will restore the plaintiff's rights. If the defendant wins the case, there is nothing more the trial court needs to do as the case is disposed of and the defendant is held not liable.

### Right to appeal

The losing party in a federal civil case has a right to appeal the verdict to the U.S. court of appeals (i.e., Federal Circuit Courts) and ask the court to review the case to determine whether the trial was conducted properly. The losing party in the state trial court has a right to appeal the verdict to the state court of appeal.

The grounds for appeal usually are that the federal district (or state) judge made an error, either in the procedure (e.g., admitting improper evidence) or interpreting the law. The government may appeal in civil cases, as any other party may. Neither party may appeal if there was no trial -- parties settled their civil case out of court.

*Notes for active learning*

## How Criminal Cases Move Through the Federal Courts

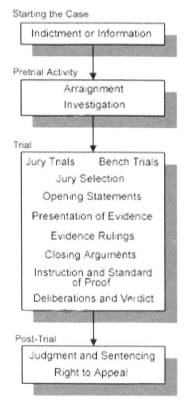

Starting the Case

Indictment or Information

Pretrial Activity

Arraignment
Investigation

Trial

Jury Trials     Bench Trials
Jury Selection
Opening Statements
Presentation of Evidence
Evidence Rulings
Closing Arguments
Instruction and Standard of Proof
Deliberations and Verdict

Post-Trial

Judgment and Sentencing
Right to Appeal

### Indictment or information

A criminal case formally begins with an indictment or information, which is a formal accusation that a person committed a crime.

An indictment may be obtained when a lawyer (i.e., prosecutor) for the executive branch of the U.S. government (i.e., U.S. attorney or assistant U.S. attorney) present evidence to a federal grand jury that, according to the government, indicates a person committed a crime.

The U.S. attorney tries to convince the grand jury that there is enough evidence to show that the person probably committed the crime and should be formally accused. If the grand jury agrees, it issues an indictment.

A grand jury is different from a trial jury or petit jury.

A grand jury determines whether the person may be tried for a crime; a petit jury listens to the evidence presented at the trial and determines whether the defendant is guilty.

*Petit* is French for "small"; petit juries usually consist of twelve jurors in criminal cases.

*Grand* is French for "large"; grand juries have from sixteen to twenty-three jurors.

Grand jury indictments are most often used for *felonies* (i.e., punishable by imprisonment of more than a year or by death) such as bank robberies or sales of illegal drugs.

Grand jury indictments are not necessary to prosecute *misdemeanors* (i.e., less serious than a felony but more serious than an infraction) and are necessary for felonies.

For lesser crimes, the U.S. attorney issues an *information* that substitutes for an indictment. For example, speeding on a highway in a national park is a misdemeanor.

An information is used when a defendant waives an indictment by a grand jury.

   

## Arraignment

After the grand jury issues the indictment, the accused (i.e., defendant) is summoned to court or arrested (if not already in custody). The next step is an arraignment, a proceeding in which the defendant is brought before a judge, told of the charges they are accused of, and asked to plead guilty or not guilty. If the defendant's plea is guilty, a time is set for the defendant to return to court to be sentenced.

If the defendant pleads "not guilty," the time is set for the trial.

A defendant may enter a plea bargain with the prosecution--usually by agreeing to plead guilty to some but not all charges or lesser charges. The prosecution drops the remaining charges.

About nine out of ten defendants in criminal cases plead guilty.

## Investigation

In a criminal case, a defense lawyer conducts a thorough investigation before trial, interviewing witnesses, visiting the crime scene, and examining physical evidence. An important part of this investigation is determining whether the evidence the government plans to use to prove its case was obtained legally.

The Fourth Amendment to the Constitution forbids unreasonable searches and seizures. To enforce this protection, the Supreme Court has decided that illegally seized evidence cannot be used at trial for most purposes.

For example, if the police seize evidence from a defendant's home without a search warrant, the lawyer for the defendant can ask the court to exclude the evidence from use at trial. The court holds a hearing to determine whether the search was unreasonable.

If the court rules that key evidence was seized illegally and cannot be used, the government often drops the charges against the defendant.

If the government has a strong case and the court ruled that the evidence was obtained legally, the defendant may decide to plead guilty rather than go to trial, where a conviction is likely.

## Deliberations and verdict

After receiving its instructions from the judge, the jury retires to the jury room to discuss the evidence and reach a verdict (a decision on the factual issues). A criminal jury verdict must be unanimous; all jurors must agree that the defendant is guilty or not guilty.

If the jurors cannot agree, the judge declares a mistrial, and the prosecutor must decide whether to ask the court to dismiss the case or have it presented to another jury.

## Judgment and sentencing

In federal criminal cases, if the jury (or judge, if there is no jury) decides that the defendant is guilty, the judge sets a date for a sentencing hearing. In federal criminal cases, the jury does not decide whether the defendant will go to prison or for how long; the judge does.

In federal death penalty cases, the jury does decide whether the defendant will receive a death sentence. Sentencing statutes passed by Congress control the judge's sentencing decision. Additionally, judges use Sentencing Guidelines, issued by the U.S. Sentencing Commission, as a source of advice as to the proper sentence. The guidelines consider the nature of the offense and the offender's criminal history.

A presentence report, prepared by one of the court's probation officers, provides the judge with information about the offender and the offense, including the sentence recommended by the guidelines. After determining the sentence, the judge signs a judgment, including the plea, the verdict, and sentence.

## Right to appeal

A defendant who is found guilty in a federal criminal trial has a right to appeal the decision to the U.S. court of appeals, that is, ask the court of appeals to review the case to determine whether the trial was conducted properly. The grounds for appeal are usually that the district judge is said to have made an error, either in a procedure (admitting improper evidence, for example) or interpreting the law.

A defendant who pled guilty may not appeal the conviction.

A defendant who pled guilty may have the right to appeal their sentence.

The government may not appeal if a defendant in a criminal case is found not guilty because the Double Jeopardy Clause of the Fifth Amendment to the Constitution provides that no person shall "be twice put in jeopardy of life or limb" for the same offense.

This reflects society's belief that, even if a subsequent trial might finally find a defendant guilty, it is not proper for the government to harass an acquitted defendant through repeated retrials.

However, the government may sometimes appeal a sentence.

*Notes for active learning*

## How Civil and Criminal Appeals Move Through the Federal Courts

Assignment of Judges

Alternative Dispute
Resolution (ADR)

Review of Lower Court
Decision

Oral Argument

Decision

The Supreme Court of
the United States

### Assignment of judges

The courts of appeals usually assign cases to a panel of three judges. The panel decides the case for the entire court. Sometimes, when the parties request it or a question of unusual importance, the judges on the appeals court assemble *en banc* (a rare event).

### Review of a lower court decision

In making its decision, the panel reviews key parts of the record. The record consists of the documents filed in the case at trial and the transcript of the trial proceedings. The panel learns about the lawyers' legal arguments from the lawyers' briefs.

Briefs are written documents that each side submits to explain its case and tell why the court should decide in its favor.

### Oral argument

If the court permits oral argument, the lawyers for each side have a limited amount of time (typically between 15 to 30 minutes) to argue (i.e., advocate and explain) their case to the judges (or justices at the highest court in the jurisdiction) in a formal courtroom session. The judges (or justices for the highest court in the jurisdiction) frequently question the attorneys about the relevant law as it applies to the facts and issues in the case before them.

A court of appeals differs from the federal trial courts. There are no jurors, witnesses, or court reporters. The lawyers for each side, but not the parties, are usually present in the courtroom.

### Decision

After the submission of briefs and oral arguments, the judges discuss the case privately, consider relevant *precedents* (court decisions from higher courts in prior cases with similar facts and legal issues), and reach a decision. Courts are required to follow precedents.

For example, a U.S. court of appeals must follow the U.S. Supreme Court's decisions; a district court must follow the decisions of the U.S. Supreme Court and the decisions of the court of appeals of its circuit.

Courts are influenced by decisions they are not required to follow, such as the decisions of other circuits. Courts follow precedent unless they set forth reasons for the diversion.

---

At least two of the three judges on the panel must agree on a decision. One judge who agrees with the decision is chosen to write an opinion, which announces and explains the decision.

If a judge on the panel disagrees with the majority's opinion, the judge may write a dissent, giving reasons for disagreeing.

Many appellate opinions are published in books of opinions, called reporters. The opinions are read carefully by other judges and lawyers looking for precedents to guide them in their cases.

The accumulated judicial opinions make up a body of law known as *case law*, which is usually an accurate predictor of how future cases will be decided.

For decisions that the judges believe are important to the parties and contribute little to the law, the appeals courts frequently use short, unsigned opinions that often are not published.

If the court of appeals decides that the trial judge incorrectly interpreted the law or followed incorrect procedures, it reverses the district court's decision.

For example, the court of appeals could hold that the district judge allowed the jury to base its decision on evidence that never should have been admitted, and thus the defendant cannot be guilty.

Most of the time, courts of appeals uphold, rather than the reverse, district court decisions.

Sometimes when a higher court reverses the decision of the district court, it sends the case back (i.e., *remand* the case) to the lower court for another trial.

For example, *Miranda v. Arizona* case (1966), the Supreme Court ruled 5-4 that Ernesto Miranda's confession could not be used as evidence because he had not been advised of his right to remain silent or of his right to have a lawyer present during questioning.

However, the government did have other evidence against him. The case was remanded for a new trial, in which the improperly obtained confession was not used as evidence, but the other evidence convicted Miranda.

### The Supreme Court of the United States

The Supreme Court is the highest in the nation. It is a different kind of appeals court; its major function is not correcting errors made by trial judges but clarifying the law in cases of national importance or when lower courts disagree about interpreting the Constitution or federal laws.

The Supreme Court does not have to hear every case that it is asked to review. Each year, losing parties ask the Supreme Court to review about 8,000 cases.

Almost all cases come to the Court as a *petition for writ of certiorari*. The court selects only about 80 to 120 of the most significant cases to review with oral arguments.

Supreme Court decisions establish a precedent for interpreting the Constitution and federal laws; holdings that state and federal courts must follow.

The power of judicial review makes the Supreme Court's role in our government vital. Judicial review is the power of a court when deciding a case to declare that a law passed by a legislature or action by the executive branch is invalid because it is inconsistent with the Constitution.

Although district courts, courts of appeals, and state courts can exercise the power of judicial review, their decisions about federal law are always subject, on appeal, to review by the Supreme Court.

When the Supreme Court declares a law unconstitutional, its decision can only be overruled by a later decision of the Supreme Court or Amendment to the Constitution.

Seven of the twenty-seven Amendments to the Constitution have invalidated the decisions of the Supreme Court. However, most Supreme Court cases do not concern the constitutionality of laws, but the interpretation of laws passed by Congress.

Although Congress has steadily increased the number of district and appeals court judges over the years, the Supreme Court has remained the same size since 1869. It consists of a Chief Justice and eight associate justices.

Like the federal court of appeals and federal district judges, the Supreme Court justices are appointed by the President with the Senate's *advice and consent*.

Unlike the judges in the courts of appeals, Supreme Court justices never sit on panels. Absent recusal, nine justices hear cases, and a majority ruling decides cases.

The Supreme Court begins its annual session, or term, on the first Monday of October. The term lasts until the Court has announced its decisions in cases where it has heard an argument that term—usually late June or early July.

During the term, the Court, sitting for two weeks at a time, hears oral arguments on Monday through Wednesday and holds private conferences to discuss the cases, reach decisions, and begin preparing the written opinions that explain its decisions.

Most decisions and opinions are released in the late spring and early summer.

## Standards of review for federal courts

| Standard of review | De novo | Clearly erroneous | Abuse of discretion |
|---|---|---|---|
| Type of decision under review | Question of the law | Question of fact | Discretionary action |
| Lower-court decision maker | Trial judge | Trial judge | Trial judge |
| Deference given to lower court | No deference | Substantial deference | Extreme deference |
| Party typically benefited | Appellant | Appellee | Appellee |
| Definition | An appellate court reviews the legal question anew and independently, without regard to the conclusions reached by the trial court. "When *de novo* review is compelled, no form of appellate deference is acceptable." *Salve Regina College v. Russell*, (1991). | A finding is 'clearly erroneous' when although there is evidence to support it, the reviewing court on the entire evidence is left with the definite and firm conviction that a mistake has been committed. *United States v. United States Gypsum Co.*, (1948) <br><br> "If the district court's account of the evidence is plausible in light of the record viewed in its entirety, the court of appeals may not reverse it even though convinced that had it been sitting as the trier of fact, it would have weighed the evidence differently. When there are two permissible views of the evidence, the factfinder's choice between them cannot be clearly erroneous." *Anderson v. Bessemer City*, (1985). | Generally, an abuse of discretion only occurs where no reasonable person could take the view adopted by the trial court. If reasonable persons could differ, no abuse of discretion can be found. *Harrington v. DeVito*, (7th Cir.1981) <br><br> Under the abuse of discretion standard, a trial court's decision will not be disturbed unless the appellate court has a definite and firm conviction that the lower court made a clear error of judgment or exceeded the bounds of permissible choice in the circumstances. We will not alter a trial court's decision unless it can be shown that the court's decision was an arbitrary, capricious, whimsical, or manifestly unreasonable judgment. *Wright v. Abbott Laboratories, Inc.*, (10th Cir. 2001). |
| Examples | Motions for summary judgment, constitutional questions, statutory interpretation | Questions regarding who did what, where, and when; questions of intent and motive; questions of ultimate fact (such as negligence) | Rule 11 sanctions, attorney's fees, courtroom management, motions to compel, injunctions, and temporary restraining orders. |

## The Constitution of the United States (*a transcription*)

### THE U.S. NATIONAL ARCHIVES & RECORDS ADMINISTRATION
www.archives.gov

The following text is a transcription of the Constitution as it was inscribed by Jacob Shallus on parchment (the document on display in the Rotunda at the National Archives Museum.) The spelling and punctuation reflect the original.

### The Constitution of the United States: A Transcription

*The following text is a transcription of the Constitution as it was inscribed by Jacob Shallus on parchment (displayed in the Rotunda at the National Archives Museum.) The authenticated text of the Constitution can be found on the website of the Government Printing Office.*

**We the People** of the United States, in Order to form a more perfect Union, establish Justice, insure domestic Tranquility, provide for the common defence, promote the general Welfare, and secure the Blessings of Liberty to ourselves and our Posterity, do ordain and establish this Constitution for the United States of America.

### Article. I

#### Section. 1.

All legislative Powers herein granted shall be vested in a Congress of the United States, which shall consist of a Senate and House of Representatives.

#### Section. 2.

The House of Representatives shall be composed of Members chosen every second Year by the People of the several States, and the Electors in each State shall have the Qualifications requisite for Electors of the most numerous Branch of the State Legislature.

No Person shall be a Representative who shall not have attained to the Age of twenty five Years, and been seven Years a Citizen of the United States, and who shall not, when elected, be an Inhabitant of that State in which he shall be chosen.

Representatives and direct Taxes shall be apportioned among the several States which may be included within this Union, according to their respective Numbers, which shall be determined by adding to the whole Number of free Persons, including those bound to Service for a Term of Years, and excluding Indians not taxed, three fifths of all other Persons. The actual Enumeration shall be made within three Years after the first Meeting of the Congress of the United States, and within every subsequent Term of ten Years, in such Manner as they shall by Law direct. The Number of Representatives shall not exceed one for every thirty Thousand, but each State shall have at Least one Representative; and until such enumeration shall be made, the State of New Hampshire shall be entitled to chuse three, Massachusetts eight, Rhode-Island and Providence

Plantations one, Connecticut five, New-York six, New Jersey four, Pennsylvania eight, Delaware one, Maryland six, Virginia ten, North Carolina five, South Carolina five, and Georgia three.

When vacancies happen in the Representation from any State, the Executive Authority thereof shall issue Writs of Election to fill such Vacancies.

The House of Representatives shall chuse their Speaker and other Officers; and shall have the sole Power of Impeachment.

**Section. 3.**

The Senate of the United States shall be composed of two Senators from each State, chosen by the Legislature thereof, for six Years; and each Senator shall have one Vote.

Immediately after they shall be assembled in Consequence of the first Election, they shall be divided as equally as may be into three Classes. The Seats of the Senators of the first Class shall be vacated at the Expiration of the second Year, of the second Class at the Expiration of the fourth Year, and of the third Class at the Expiration of the sixth Year, so that one third may be chosen every second Year; and if Vacancies happen by Resignation, or otherwise, during the Recess of the Legislature of any State, the Executive thereof may make temporary Appointments until the next Meeting of the Legislature, which shall then fill such Vacancies.

No Person shall be a Senator who shall not have attained to the Age of thirty Years, and been nine Years a Citizen of the United States, and who shall not, when elected, be an Inhabitant of that State for which he shall be chosen.

The Vice President of the United States shall be President of the Senate, but shall have no Vote, unless they be equally divided.

The Senate shall chuse their other Officers, and also a President pro tempore, in the Absence of the Vice President, or when he shall exercise the Office of President of the United States.

The Senate shall have the sole Power to try all Impeachments. When sitting for that Purpose, they shall be on Oath or Affirmation. When the President of the United States is tried, the Chief Justice shall preside: And no Person shall be convicted without the Concurrence of two thirds of the Members present.

Judgment in Cases of Impeachment shall not extend further than to removal from Office, and disqualification to hold and enjoy any Office of honor, Trust or Profit under the United States: but the Party convicted shall nevertheless be liable and subject to Indictment, Trial, Judgment and Punishment, according to Law.

**Section. 4.**

The Times, Places and Manner of holding Elections for Senators and Representatives, shall be prescribed in each State by the Legislature thereof; but the Congress may at any time by Law make or alter such Regulations, except as to the Places of chusing Senators.

The Congress shall assemble at least once in every Year, and such Meeting shall be on the first Monday in December, unless they shall by Law appoint a different Day.

## Section. 5.

Each House shall be the Judge of the Elections, Returns and Qualifications of its own Members, and a Majority of each shall constitute a Quorum to do Business; but a smaller Number may adjourn from day to day, and may be authorized to compel the Attendance of absent Members, in such Manner, and under such Penalties as each House may provide.

Each House may determine the Rules of its Proceedings, punish its Members for disorderly Behaviour, and, with the Concurrence of two thirds, expel a Member.

Each House shall keep a Journal of its Proceedings, and from time to time publish the same, excepting such Parts as may in their Judgment require Secrecy; and the Yeas and Nays of the Members of either House on any question shall, at the Desire of one fifth of those Present, be entered on the Journal.

Neither House, during the Session of Congress, shall, without the Consent of the other, adjourn for more than three days, nor to any other Place than that in which the two Houses shall be sitting.

## Section. 6.

The Senators and Representatives shall receive a Compensation for their Services, to be ascertained by Law, and paid out of the Treasury of the United States. They shall in all Cases, except Treason, Felony and Breach of the Peace, be privileged from Arrest during their Attendance at the Session of their respective Houses, and in going to and returning from the same; and for any Speech or Debate in either House, they shall not be questioned in any other Place.

No Senator or Representative shall, during the Time for which he was elected, be appointed to any civil Office under the Authority of the United States, which shall have been created, or the Emoluments whereof shall have been encreased during such time; and no Person holding any Office under the United States, shall be a Member of either House during his Continuance in Office.

## Section. 7.

All Bills for raising Revenue shall originate in the House of Representatives; but the Senate may propose or concur with Amendments as on other Bills.

Every Bill which shall have passed the House of Representatives and the Senate, shall, before it become a Law, be presented to the President of the United States; If he approves he shall sign it, but if not he shall return it, with his Objections to that House in which it shall have originated, who shall enter the Objections at large on their Journal, and proceed to reconsider it. If after such Reconsideration two thirds of that House shall agree to pass the Bill, it shall be sent, together with the Objections, to the other House, by which it shall likewise be reconsidered, and if approved by two thirds of that House, it shall become a Law. But in all such Cases the Votes of both Houses shall be determined by yeas and Nays, and the Names of the Persons voting for and against the Bill shall be entered on the Journal of each House respectively. If any Bill shall not be returned by the President within ten Days (Sundays excepted) after it shall have been presented to him, the Same shall be a Law, in like Manner as if he had signed it, unless the Congress by their Adjournment prevent its Return, in which Case it shall not be a Law.

Every Order, Resolution, or Vote to which the Concurrence of the Senate and House of Representatives may be necessary (except on a question of Adjournment) shall be presented to the President of the United States; and before the Same shall take Effect, shall be approved by him, or being disapproved by him, shall be repassed by two thirds of the Senate and House of Representatives, according to the Rules and Limitations prescribed in the Case of a Bill.

**Section. 8.**

The Congress shall have Power To lay and collect Taxes, Duties, Imposts and Excises, to pay the Debts and provide for the common Defence and general Welfare of the United States; but all Duties, Imposts and Excises shall be uniform throughout the United States;

To borrow Money on the credit of the United States;

To regulate Commerce with foreign Nations, and among the several States, and with the Indian Tribes;

To establish an uniform Rule of Naturalization, and uniform Laws on the subject of Bankruptcies throughout the United States;

To coin Money, regulate the Value thereof, and of foreign Coin, and fix the Standard of Weights and Measures;

To provide for the Punishment of counterfeiting the Securities and current Coin of the United States;

To establish Post Offices and post Roads;

To promote the Progress of Science and useful Arts, by securing for limited Times to Authors and Inventors the exclusive Right to their respective Writings and Discoveries;

To constitute Tribunals inferior to the Supreme Court;

To define and punish Piracies and Felonies committed on the high Seas, and Offences against the Law of Nations;

To declare War, grant Letters of Marque and Reprisal, and make Rules concerning Captures on Land and Water;

To raise and support Armies, but no Appropriation of Money to that Use shall be for a longer Term than two Years;

To provide and maintain a Navy;

To make Rules for the Government and Regulation of the land and naval Forces;

To provide for calling forth the Militia to execute the Laws of the Union, suppress Insurrections and repel Invasions;

To provide for organizing, arming, and disciplining, the Militia, and for governing such Part of them as may be employed in the Service of the United States, reserving to the States respectively, the Appointment of the Officers, and the Authority of training the Militia according to the discipline prescribed by Congress;

To exercise exclusive Legislation in all Cases whatsoever, over such District (not exceeding ten Miles square) as may, by Cession of particular States, and the Acceptance of Congress, become the Seat of the Government of the United States, and to exercise like Authority over all Places purchased by the Consent of the Legislature of the State in which the Same shall be, for the Erection of Forts, Magazines, Arsenals, dock-Yards, and other needful Buildings;—And

To make all Laws which shall be necessary and proper for carrying into Execution the foregoing Powers, and all other Powers vested by this Constitution in the Government of the United States, or in any Department or Officer thereof.

### Section. 9.

The Migration or Importation of such Persons as any of the States now existing shall think proper to admit, shall not be prohibited by the Congress prior to the Year one thousand eight hundred and eight, but a Tax or duty may be imposed on such Importation, not exceeding ten dollars for each Person.

The Privilege of the Writ of Habeas Corpus shall not be suspended, unless when in Cases of Rebellion or Invasion the public Safety may require it.

No Bill of Attainder or ex post facto Law shall be passed.

No Capitation, or other direct, Tax shall be laid, unless in Proportion to the Census or enumeration herein before directed to be taken.

No Tax or Duty shall be laid on Articles exported from any State.

No Preference shall be given by any Regulation of Commerce or Revenue to the Ports of one State over those of another: nor shall Vessels bound to, or from, one State, be obliged to enter, clear, or pay Duties in another.

No Money shall be drawn from the Treasury, but in Consequence of Appropriations made by Law; and a regular Statement and Account of the Receipts and Expenditures of all public Money shall be published from time to time.

No Title of Nobility shall be granted by the United States: And no Person holding any Office of Profit or Trust under them, shall, without the Consent of the Congress, accept of any present, Emolument, Office, or Title, of any kind whatever, from any King, Prince, or foreign State.

### Section. 10.

No State shall enter into any Treaty, Alliance, or Confederation; grant Letters of Marque and Reprisal; coin Money; emit Bills of Credit; make any Thing but gold and silver Coin a Tender in Payment of Debts; pass any Bill of Attainder, ex post facto Law, or Law impairing the Obligation of Contracts, or grant any Title of Nobility.

No State shall, without the Consent of the Congress, lay any Imposts or Duties on Imports or Exports, except what may be absolutely necessary for executing it's inspection Laws: and the net

Produce of all Duties and Imposts, laid by any State on Imports or Exports, shall be for the Use of the Treasury of the United States; and all such Laws shall be subject to the Revision and Controul of the Congress.

No State shall, without the Consent of Congress, lay any Duty of Tonnage, keep Troops, or Ships of War in time of Peace, enter into any Agreement or Compact with another State, or with a foreign Power, or engage in War, unless actually invaded, or in such imminent Danger as will not admit of delay.

---

## Article. II

**Section. 1.**

The executive Power shall be vested in a President of the United States of America. He shall hold his Office during the Term of four Years, and, together with the Vice President, chosen for the same Term, be elected, as follows

Each State shall appoint, in such Manner as the Legislature thereof may direct, a Number of Electors, equal to the whole Number of Senators and Representatives to which the State may be entitled in the Congress: but no Senator or Representative, or Person holding an Office of Trust or Profit under the United States, shall be appointed an Elector.

The Electors shall meet in their respective States, and vote by Ballot for two Persons, of whom one at least shall not be an Inhabitant of the same State with themselves. And they shall make a List of all the Persons voted for, and of the Number of Votes for each; which List they shall sign and certify, and transmit sealed to the Seat of the Government of the United States, directed to the President of the Senate. The President of the Senate shall, in the Presence of the Senate and House of Representatives, open all the Certificates, and the Votes shall then be counted. The Person having the greatest Number of Votes shall be the President, if such Number be a Majority of the whole Number of Electors appointed; and if there be more than one who have such Majority, and have an equal Number of Votes, then the House of Representatives shall immediately chuse by Ballot one of them for President; and if no Person have a Majority, then from the five highest on the List the said House shall in like Manner chuse the President. But in chusing the President, the Votes shall be taken by States, the Representation from each State having one Vote; A quorum for this Purpose shall consist of a Member or Members from two thirds of the States, and a Majority of all the States shall be necessary to a Choice. In every Case, after the Choice of the President, the Person having the greatest Number of Votes of the Electors shall be the Vice President. But if there should remain two or more who have equal Votes, the Senate shall chuse from them by Ballot the Vice President.

The Congress may determine the Time of chusing the Electors, and the Day on which they shall give their Votes; which Day shall be the same throughout the United States.

No Person except a natural born Citizen, or a Citizen of the United States, at the time of the Adoption of this Constitution, shall be eligible to the Office of President; neither shall any Person be eligible to that Office who shall not have attained to the Age of thirty five Years, and been fourteen Years a Resident within the United States.

In Case of the Removal of the President from Office, or of his Death, Resignation, or Inability to discharge the Powers and Duties of the said Office, the Same shall devolve on the Vice President, and the Congress may by Law provide for the Case of Removal, Death, Resignation or Inability, both of the President and Vice President, declaring what Officer shall then act as President, and such Officer shall act accordingly, until the Disability be removed, or a President shall be elected

The President shall, at stated Times, receive for his Services, a Compensation, which shall neither be encreased nor diminished during the Period for which he shall have been elected, and he shall not receive within that Period any other Emolument from the United States, or any of them.

Before he enters on the Execution of his Office, he shall take the following Oath or Affirmation:—"I do solemnly swear (or affirm) that I will faithfully execute the Office of President of the United States, and will to the best of my Ability, preserve, protect and defend the Constitution of the United States."

## Section. 2.

The President shall be Commander in Chief of the Army and Navy of the United States, and of the Militia of the several States, when called into the actual Service of the United States; he may require the Opinion, in writing, of the principal Officer in each of the executive Departments, upon any Subject relating to the Duties of their respective Offices, and he shall have Power to grant Reprieves and Pardons for Offences against the United States, except in Cases of Impeachment.

He shall have Power, by and with the Advice and Consent of the Senate, to make Treaties, provided two thirds of the Senators present concur; and he shall nominate, and by and with the Advice and Consent of the Senate, shall appoint Ambassadors, other public Ministers and Consuls, Judges of the supreme Court, and all other Officers of the United States, whose Appointments are not herein otherwise provided for, and which shall be established by Law: but the Congress may by Law vest the Appointment of such inferior Officers, as they think proper, in the President alone, in the Courts of Law, or in the Heads of Departments.

The President shall have Power to fill up all Vacancies that may happen during the Recess of the Senate, by granting Commissions which shall expire at the End of their next Session.

## Section. 3.

He shall from time to time give to the Congress Information of the State of the Union, and recommend to their Consideration such Measures as he shall judge necessary and expedient; he may, on extraordinary Occasions, convene both Houses, or either of them, and in Case of Disagreement between them, with Respect to the Time of Adjournment, he may adjourn them to such Time as he shall think proper; he shall receive Ambassadors and other public Ministers; he shall take Care that the Laws be faithfully executed, and shall Commission all the Officers of the United States.

**Section. 4.**

The President, Vice President and all civil Officers of the United States, shall be removed from Office on Impeachment for, and Conviction of, Treason, Bribery, or other high Crimes and Misdemeanors.

---

## Article III

**Section. 1.**

The judicial Power of the United States, shall be vested in one supreme Court, and in such inferior Courts as the Congress may from time to time ordain and establish. The Judges, both of the supreme and inferior Courts, shall hold their Offices during good Behaviour, and shall, at stated Times, receive for their Services, a Compensation, which shall not be diminished during their Continuance in Office.

**Section. 2.**

The judicial Power shall extend to all Cases, in Law and Equity, arising under this Constitution, the Laws of the United States, and Treaties made, or which shall be made, under their Authority;—to all Cases affecting Ambassadors, other public Ministers and Consuls;—to all Cases of admiralty and maritime Jurisdiction;—to Controversies to which the United States shall be a Party;—to Controversies between two or more States;—between a State and Citizens of another State,—between Citizens of different States,—between Citizens of the same State claiming Lands under Grants of different States, and between a State, or the Citizens thereof, and foreign States, Citizens or Subjects.

In all Cases affecting Ambassadors, other public Ministers and Consuls, and those in which a State shall be Party, the supreme Court shall have original Jurisdiction. In all the other Cases before mentioned, the supreme Court shall have appellate Jurisdiction, both as to Law and Fact, with such Exceptions, and under such Regulations as the Congress shall make.

The Trial of all Crimes, except in Cases of Impeachment, shall be by Jury; and such Trial shall be held in the State where the said Crimes shall have been committed; but when not committed within any State, the Trial shall be at such Place or Places as the Congress may by Law have directed.

**Section. 3.**

Treason against the United States, shall consist only in levying War against them, or in adhering to their Enemies, giving them Aid and Comfort. No Person shall be convicted of Treason unless on the Testimony of two Witnesses to the same overt Act, or on Confession in open Court.

The Congress shall have Power to declare the Punishment of Treason, but no Attainder of Treason shall work Corruption of Blood, or Forfeiture except during the Life of the Person attainted.

## Article. IV

### Section. 1.

Full Faith and Credit shall be given in each State to the public Acts, Records, and judicial Proceedings of every other State. And the Congress may by general Laws prescribe the Manner in which such Acts, Records and Proceedings shall be proved, and the Effect thereof.

### Section. 2.

The Citizens of each State shall be entitled to all Privileges and Immunities of Citizens in the several States.

A Person charged in any State with Treason, Felony, or other Crime, who shall flee from Justice, and be found in another State, shall on Demand of the executive Authority of the State from which he fled, be delivered up, to be removed to the State having Jurisdiction of the Crime.

No Person held to Service or Labour in one State, under the Laws thereof, escaping into another, shall, in Consequence of any Law or Regulation therein, be discharged from such Service or Labour, but shall be delivered up on Claim of the Party to whom such Service or Labour may be due.

### Section. 3.

New States may be admitted by the Congress into this Union; but no new State shall be formed or erected within the Jurisdiction of any other State; nor any State be formed by the Junction of two or more States, or Parts of States, without the Consent of the Legislatures of the States concerned as well as of the Congress.

The Congress shall have Power to dispose of and make all needful Rules and Regulations respecting the Territory or other Property belonging to the United States; and nothing in this Constitution shall be so construed as to Prejudice any Claims of the United States, or of any particular State.

### Section. 4.

The United States shall guarantee to every State in this Union a Republican Form of Government, and shall protect each of them against Invasion; and on Application of the Legislature, or of the Executive (when the Legislature cannot be convened), against domestic Violence.

## Article. V

The Congress, whenever two thirds of both Houses shall deem it necessary, shall propose Amendments to this Constitution, or, on the Application of the Legislatures of two thirds of the several States, shall call a Convention for proposing Amendments, which, in either Case, shall be valid to all Intents and Purposes, as Part of this Constitution, when ratified by the Legislatures of three fourths of the several States, or by Conventions in three fourths thereof, as the one or the other Mode of Ratification may be proposed by the Congress; Provided that no Amendment which may be made prior to the Year One thousand eight hundred and eight shall in any Manner affect the first and fourth Clauses in the Ninth Section of the first Article; and that no State, without its Consent, shall be deprived of its equal Suffrage in the Senate.

## Article. VI

All Debts contracted and Engagements entered into, before the Adoption of this Constitution, shall be as valid against the United States under this Constitution, as under the Confederation.

This Constitution, and the Laws of the United States which shall be made in Pursuance thereof; and all Treaties made, or which shall be made, under the Authority of the United States, shall be the supreme Law of the Land; and the Judges in every State shall be bound thereby, any Thing in the Constitution or Laws of any State to the Contrary notwithstanding.

The Senators and Representatives before mentioned, and the Members of the several State Legislatures, and all executive and judicial Officers, both of the United States and of the several States, shall be bound by Oath or Affirmation, to support this Constitution; but no religious Test shall ever be required as a Qualification to any Office or public Trust under the United States.

## Article. VII

The Ratification of the Conventions of nine States, shall be sufficient for the Establishment of this Constitution between the States so ratifying the Same.

The Word, "the," being interlined between the seventh and eighth Lines of the first Page, The Word "Thirty" being partly written on an Erazure in the fifteenth Line of the first Page, The Words "is tried" being interlined between the thirty second and thirty third Lines of the first Page and the Word "the" being interlined between the forty third and forty fourth Lines of the second Page.

Attest William Jackson Secretary, done in Convention by the Unanimous Consent of the States present the Seventeenth Day of September in the Year of our Lord one thousand seven hundred and Eighty seven and of the Independance of the United States of America the Twelfth In witness whereof We have hereunto subscribed our Names, G°. Washington, *Presidt and deputy from Virginia*

**Delaware**
*Geo: Read*
*Gunning Bedford jun*
*John Dickinson*
*Richard Bassett*
*Jaco: Broom*

**Maryland**
*James McHenry*
*Dan of St Thos.*
*Jenifer*
*Danl. Carroll*

**Virginia**
*John Blair*
*James Madison Jr.*

**North Carolina**
*Wm. Blount*
*Richd. Dobbs*
*Spaight*
*Hu Williamson*

**South Carolina**
*J. Rutledge*
*Charles Cotesworth*
*Pinckney*
*Charles Pinckney*
*Pierce Butler*

**Georgia**
*William Few*
*Abr Baldwin*

**New Hampshire**
*John Langdon*
*Nicholas Gilman*

**Massachusetts**
*Nathaniel Gorham*
*Rufus King*

**Connecticut**
*Wm. Saml. Johnson*
*Roger Sherman*

**New York**
*Alexander Hamilton*

**New Jersey**
*Wil: Livingston*
*David Brearley*
*Wm. Paterson*
*Jona: Dayton*

**Pensylvania**
*B Franklin*
*Thomas Mifflin*
*Robt. Morris*
*Geo. Clymer*
*Thos. FitzSimons*
*Jared Ingersoll*
*James Wilson*
*Gouv Morris*

## Enactment of the Bill of Rights of the United States of America (1791)

The first ten Amendments to the Constitution make up the Bill of Rights. Written by James Madison in response to calls from several states for greater constitutional protection for individual liberties, the Bill of Rights lists specific prohibitions on governmental power. The Virginia Declaration of Rights, written by George Mason, strongly influenced Madison.

One of the contention points between Federalists and Anti-Federalists was the Constitution's lack of a bill of rights that would place specific limits on government power.

Federalists argued that the Constitution did not need a bill of rights because the people and the states kept powers not explicitly given to the federal government.

Anti-Federalists held that a *bill of rights* was necessary to safeguard individual liberty.

Madison, then a member of the U.S. House of Representatives, went through the Constitution itself, making changes where he thought most appropriate.

Several Representatives, led by Roger Sherman, objected that Congress had no authority to change the wording of the Constitution. Therefore, Madison's changes were presented as a list of amendments that would follow Article VII.

The House approved 17 amendments. Of these 17, the Senate approved 12. Those 12 were sent to the states for approval in August of 1789. Of those 12 proposed amendments, 10 were quickly ratified. Virginia's legislature became the last to ratify the Amendments on December 15, 1791. These Amendments are the Bill of Rights.

The Bill of Rights is a list of limits on government power. For example, what the Founders saw as the natural right of individuals to speak and worship freely was protected by the First Amendment's prohibitions on Congress from making laws establishing a religion or abridging freedom of speech.

Another example is the natural right to be free from the government's unreasonable intrusion in one's home was safeguarded by the Fourth Amendment's warrant requirements.

Other precursors to the Bill of Rights include English documents such as the Magna Carta[1], the Petition of Rights, the English Bill of Rights, and the Massachusetts Body of Liberties.

The Magna Carta illustrates Compact Theory[1] as well as initial strides toward limited government. Its provisions address individual rights and political rights. Latin for "Great Charter," the Magna Carta was written by Barons in Runnymede, England, and forced on the King.

Although the protections were generally limited to the prerogatives of the Barons, the Magna Carta embodied the general principle that the King accepted limitations on his rule. These included the fundamental acknowledgment that the king was not above the law.

Included in the Magna Carta are protections for the English church, petitioning the king, freedom from the forced quarter of troops and unreasonable searches, due process and fair trial protections, and freedom from excessive fines. These protections can be found in the First, Third, Fourth, Fifth, Sixth, and Eighth Amendments to the Constitution.

The Magna Carta is the oldest compact in England. The Mayflower Compact, the Fundamental Orders of Connecticut, and the Albany Plan are examples from the American colonies.

The Articles of Confederation was a compact among the states, and the Constitution creates a compact based on a federal system between the national government, state governments, and the people. The Hayne-Webster Debate focused on the compact created by the Constitution.

[1] Philosophers including Thomas Hobbes, John Locke, and Jean-Jacques Rousseau theorized that peoples' condition in a "state of nature" (that is, outside of society) is one of freedom, but that freedom inevitably degrades into war, chaos, or debilitating competition without the benefit of a system of laws and government. They reasoned, therefore, that for their happiness, individuals willingly trade some of their natural freedom in exchange for the protections provided by the government.

## The Bill of Rights: Amendments I–X

### Amendment I

Congress shall make no law respecting an establishment of religion, or prohibiting the free exercise thereof; or abridging the freedom of speech, or of the press; or the right of the people peaceably to assemble, and to petition the government for a redress of grievances.

### Amendment II

A well regulated militia, being necessary to the security of a free state, the right of the people to keep and bear arms, shall not be infringed.

### Amendment III

No soldier shall, in time of peace be quartered in any house, without the consent of the owner, nor in time of war, but in a manner to be prescribed by law.

### Amendment IV

The right of the people to be secure in their persons, houses, papers, and effects, against unreasonable searches and seizures, shall not be violated, and no warrants shall issue, but upon probable cause, supported by oath or affirmation, and particularly describing the place to be searched, and the persons or things to be seized.

### Amendment V

No person shall be held to answer for a capital, or otherwise infamous crime, unless on a presentment or indictment of a grand jury, except in cases arising in the land or naval forces, or in the militia, when in actual service in time of war or public danger; nor shall any person be subject for the same offense to be twice put in jeopardy of life or limb; nor shall be compelled in any criminal case to be a witness against himself, nor be deprived of life, liberty, or property, without due process of law; nor shall private property be taken for public use, without just compensation.

### Amendment VI

In all criminal prosecutions, the accused shall enjoy the right to a speedy and public trial, by an impartial jury of the state and district wherein the crime shall have been committed, which district shall have been previously ascertained by law, and to be informed of the nature and cause of the accusation; to be confronted with the witnesses against him; to have compulsory process for obtaining witnesses in his favor, and to have the assistance of counsel for his defense.

### Amendment VII

In suits at common law, where the value in controversy shall exceed twenty dollars, the right of trial by jury shall be preserved, and no fact tried by a jury, shall be otherwise reexamined in any court of the United States, than according to the rules of the common law.

## Amendment VIII

Excessive bail shall not be required, nor excessive fines imposed, nor cruel and unusual punishments inflicted.

## Amendment IX

The enumeration in the Constitution, of certain rights, shall not be construed to deny or disparage others retained by the people.

## Amendment X

The powers not delegated to the United States by the Constitution, nor prohibited by it to the states, are reserved to the states respectively, or to the people.

## Constitutional Amendments XI–XXVII

### AMENDMENT XI

*Passed by Congress March 4, 1794. Ratified February 7, 1795.*

**Note**: Article III, section 2, of the Constitution was modified by amendment 11.

The Judicial power of the United States shall not be construed to extend to any suit in law or equity, commenced or prosecuted against one of the United States by Citizens of another State, or by Citizens or Subjects of any Foreign State.

### AMENDMENT XII

*Passed by Congress December 9, 1803. Ratified June 15, 1804.*

**Note**: A portion of Article II, section 1 of the Constitution was superseded by the 12th amendment.

The Electors shall meet in their respective states and vote by ballot for President and Vice-President, one of whom, at least, shall not be an inhabitant of the same state with themselves; they shall name in their ballots the person voted for as President, and in distinct ballots the person voted for as Vice-President, and they shall make distinct lists of all persons voted for as President, and of all persons voted for as Vice-President, and of the number of votes for each, which lists they shall sign and certify, and transmit sealed to the seat of the government of the United States, directed to the President of the Senate; -- the President of the Senate shall, in the presence of the Senate and House of Representatives, open all the certificates and the votes shall then be counted; -- The person having the greatest number of votes for President, shall be the President, if such number be a majority of the whole number of Electors appointed; and if no person have such majority, then from the persons having the highest numbers not exceeding three on the list of those voted for as President, the House of Representatives shall choose immediately, by ballot, the President. But in choosing the President, the votes shall be taken by states, the representation from each state having one vote; a quorum for this purpose shall consist of a member or members from two-thirds of the states, and a majority of all the states shall be necessary to a choice. [And if the House of Representatives shall not choose a President whenever the right of choice shall devolve upon them, before the fourth day of March next following, then the Vice-President shall act as President, as in case of the death or other constitutional disability of the President. --]* The person having the greatest number of votes as Vice-President, shall be the Vice-President, if such number be a majority of the whole number of Electors appointed, and if no person have a majority, then from the two highest numbers on the list, the Senate shall choose the Vice-President; a quorum for the purpose shall consist of two-thirds of the whole number of Senators, and a majority of the whole number shall be necessary to a choice. But no person constitutionally ineligible to the office of President shall be eligible to that of Vice-President of the United States.

*Superseded by section 3 of the 20th Amendment.*

## AMENDMENT XIII

*Passed by Congress January 31, 1865. Ratified December 6, 1865.*

**Note**: A portion of Article IV, section 2, of the Constitution was superseded by the 13th amendment.

### Section 1.

Neither slavery nor involuntary servitude, except as a punishment for crime whereof the party shall have been duly convicted, shall exist within the United States, or any place subject to their jurisdiction.

### Section 2.

Congress shall have power to enforce this article by appropriate legislation.

---

## AMENDMENT XIV

*Passed by Congress June 13, 1866. Ratified July 9, 1868.*

**Note**: Article I, section 2, of the Constitution was modified by section 2 of the 14th amendment.

### Section 1.

All persons born or naturalized in the United States, and subject to the jurisdiction thereof, are citizens of the United States and of the State wherein they reside. No State shall make or enforce any law which shall abridge the privileges or immunities of citizens of the United States; nor shall any State deprive any person of life, liberty, or property, without due process of law; nor deny to any person within its jurisdiction the equal protection of the laws.

### Section 2.

Representatives shall be apportioned among the several States according to their respective numbers, counting the whole number of persons in each State, excluding Indians not taxed. But when the right to vote at any election for the choice of electors for President and Vice-President of the United States, Representatives in Congress, the Executive and Judicial officers of a State, or the members of the Legislature thereof, is denied to any of the male inhabitants of such State, being twenty-one years of age,* and citizens of the United States, or in any way abridged, except for participation in rebellion, or other crime, the basis of representation therein shall be reduced in the proportion which the number of such male citizens shall bear to the whole number of male citizens twenty-one years of age in such State.

### Section 3.

No person shall be a Senator or Representative in Congress, or elector of President and Vice-President, or hold any office, civil or military, under the United States, or under any State, who, having previously taken an oath, as a member of Congress, or as an officer of the United States, or as a member of any State legislature, or as an executive or judicial officer of any State, to support the Constitution of the United States, shall have engaged in insurrection or rebellion against the same, or given aid or comfort to the enemies thereof. But Congress may by a vote of two-thirds of each House, remove such disability.

**Section 4.**

The validity of the public debt of the United States, authorized by law, including debts incurred for payment of pensions and bounties for services in suppressing insurrection or rebellion, shall not be questioned. But neither the United States nor any State shall assume or pay any debt or obligation incurred in aid of insurrection or rebellion against the United States, or any claim for the loss or emancipation of any slave; but all such debts, obligations and claims shall be held illegal and void.

**Section 5.**

The Congress shall have the power to enforce, by appropriate legislation, the provisions of this article.

*\*Changed by section 1 of the 26th Amendment.*

## AMENDMENT XV

*Passed by Congress February 26, 1869. Ratified February 3, 1870.*

**Section 1.**

The right of citizens of the United States to vote shall not be denied or abridged by the United States or by any State on account of race, color, or previous condition of servitude.

**Section 2.**

The Congress shall have the power to enforce this article by appropriate legislation.

## AMENDMENT XVI

*Passed by Congress July 2, 1909. Ratified February 3, 1913.*

**Note**: Article I, section 9, of the Constitution was modified by amendment 16.

The Congress shall have power to lay and collect taxes on incomes, from whatever source derived, without apportionment among the several States, and without regard to any census or enumeration.

## AMENDMENT XVII

*Passed by Congress May 13, 1912. Ratified April 8, 1913.*

**Note**: Article I, section 3, of the Constitution was modified by the 17th Amendment.

The Senate of the United States shall be composed of two Senators from each State, elected by the people thereof, for six years; and each Senator shall have one vote. The electors in each State shall have the qualifications requisite for electors of the most numerous branch of the State legislatures.

When vacancies happen in the representation of any State in the Senate, the executive authority of such State shall issue writs of election to fill such vacancies: *Provided*, That the legislature of any State may empower the executive thereof to make temporary appointments until the people fill the vacancies by election as the legislature may direct.

This amendment shall not be so construed as to affect the election or term of any Senator chosen before it becomes valid as part of the Constitution.

## AMENDMENT XVIII

*Passed by Congress December 18, 1917. Ratified January 16, 1919. Repealed by Amendment 21.*

**Section 1.**

After one year from the ratification of this article the manufacture, sale, or transportation of intoxicating liquors within, the importation thereof into, or the exportation thereof from the United States and all territory subject to the jurisdiction thereof for beverage purposes is hereby prohibited.

**Section 2.**

The Congress and the several States shall have concurrent power to enforce this article by appropriate legislation.

**Section 3.**

This article shall be inoperative unless it shall have been ratified as an amendment to the Constitution by the legislatures of the several States, as provided in the Constitution, within seven years from the date of the submission hereof to the States by the Congress.

---

## AMENDMENT XIX

*Passed by Congress June 4, 1919. Ratified August 18, 1920.*

The right of citizens of the United States to vote shall not be denied or abridged by the United States or by any State on account of sex.

Congress shall have power to enforce this article by appropriate legislation.

---

## AMENDMENT XX

*Passed by Congress March 2, 1932. Ratified January 23, 1933.*

**Note**: Article I, section 4, of the Constitution was modified by section 2 of this Amendment. In addition, a portion of the 12th Amendment was superseded by section 3.

**Section 1.**

The terms of the President and the Vice President shall end at noon on the 20th day of January, and the terms of Senators and Representatives at noon on the 3d day of January, of the years in which such terms would have ended if this article had not been ratified; and the terms of their successors shall then begin.

**Section 2.**

The Congress shall assemble at least once in every year, and such meeting shall begin at noon on the 3d day of January, unless they shall by law appoint a different day.

## Section 3.

If, at the time fixed for the beginning of the term of the President, the President elect shall have died, the Vice President elect shall become President. If a President shall not have been chosen before the time fixed for the beginning of his term, or if the President elect shall have failed to qualify, then the Vice President elect shall act as President until a President shall have qualified; and the Congress may by law provide for the case wherein neither a President elect nor a Vice President elect shall have qualified, declaring who shall then act as President, or the manner in which one who is to act shall be selected, and such person shall act accordingly until a President or Vice President shall have qualified.

## Section 4.

The Congress may by law provide for the case of the death of any of the persons from whom the House of Representatives may choose a President whenever the right of choice shall have devolved upon them, and for the case of the death of any of the persons from whom the Senate may choose a Vice President whenever the right of choice shall have devolved upon them.

## Section 5.

Sections 1 and 2 shall take effect on the 15th day of October following the ratification of this article.

## Section 6.

This article shall be inoperative unless it shall have been ratified as an amendment to the Constitution by the legislatures of three-fourths of the several States within seven years from the date of its submission.

---

## AMENDMENT XXI

*Passed by Congress February 20, 1933. Ratified December 5, 1933.*

## Section 1.

The eighteenth article of amendment to the Constitution of the United States is hereby repealed.

## Section 2.

The transportation or importation into any State, Territory, or possession of the United States for delivery or use therein of intoxicating liquors, in violation of the laws thereof, is hereby prohibited.

## Section 3.

This article shall be inoperative unless it shall have been ratified as an amendment to the Constitution by conventions in the several States, as provided in the Constitution, within seven years from the date of the submission hereof to the States by the Congress.

---

## AMENDMENT XXII

*Passed by Congress March 21, 1947. Ratified February 27, 1951.*

**Section 1.**

No person shall be elected to the office of the President more than twice, and no person who has held the office of President, or acted as President, for more than two years of a term to which some other person was elected President shall be elected to the office of the President more than once. But this Article shall not apply to any person holding the office of President when this Article was proposed by the Congress, and shall not prevent any person who may be holding the office of President, or acting as President, during the term within which this Article becomes operative from holding the office of President or acting as President during the remainder of such term.

**Section 2.**

This article shall be inoperative unless it shall have been ratified as an amendment to the Constitution by the legislatures of three-fourths of the several States within seven years from the date of its submission to the States by the Congress.

## AMENDMENT XXIII

*Passed by Congress June 16, 1960. Ratified March 29, 1961.*

**Section 1.**

The District constituting the seat of Government of the United States shall appoint in such manner as the Congress may direct:

A number of electors of President and Vice President equal to the whole number of Senators and Representatives in Congress to which the District would be entitled if it were a State, but in no event more than the least populous State; they shall be in addition to those appointed by the States, but they shall be considered, for the purposes of the election of President and Vice President, to be electors appointed by a State; and they shall meet in the District and perform such duties as provided by the twelfth article of amendment.

**Section 2.**

The Congress shall have power to enforce this article by appropriate legislation.

## AMENDMENT XXIV

*Passed by Congress August 27, 1962. Ratified January 23, 1964.*

**Section 1.**

The right of citizens of the United States to vote in any primary or other election for President or Vice President, for electors for President or Vice President, or for Senator or Representative in Congress, shall not be denied or abridged by the United States or any State by reason of failure to pay any poll tax or other tax.

## Section 2.

The Congress shall have power to enforce this article by appropriate legislation.

---

## AMENDMENT XXV

*Passed by Congress July 6, 1965. Ratified February 10, 1967.*

**Note**: Article II, section 1, of the Constitution was affected by the 25th amendment.

### Section 1.

In case of the removal of the President from office or of his death or resignation, the Vice President shall become President.

### Section 2.

Whenever there is a vacancy in the office of the Vice President, the President shall nominate a Vice President who shall take office upon confirmation by a majority vote of both Houses of Congress.

### Section 3.

Whenever the President transmits to the President pro tempore of the Senate and the Speaker of the House of Representatives his written declaration that he is unable to discharge the powers and duties of his office, and until he transmits to them a written declaration to the contrary, such powers and duties shall be discharged by the Vice President as Acting President.

### Section 4.

Whenever the Vice President and a majority of either the principal officers of the executive departments or of such other body as Congress may by law provide, transmit to the President pro tempore of the Senate and the Speaker of the House of Representatives their written declaration that the President is unable to discharge the powers and duties of his office, the Vice President shall immediately assume the powers and duties of the office as Acting President.

Thereafter, when the President transmits to the President pro tempore of the Senate and the Speaker of the House of Representatives his written declaration that no inability exists, he shall resume the powers and duties of his office unless the Vice President and a majority of either the principal officers of the executive department or of such other body as Congress may by law provide, transmit within four days to the President pro tempore of the Senate and the Speaker of the House of Representatives their written declaration that the President is unable to discharge the powers and duties of his office. Thereupon Congress shall decide the issue, assembling within forty-eight hours for that purpose if not in session. If the Congress, within twenty-one days after receipt of the latter written declaration, or, if Congress is not in session, within twenty-one days after Congress is required to assemble, determines by two-thirds vote of both Houses that the President is unable to discharge the powers and duties of his office, the Vice President shall continue to discharge the same as Acting President; otherwise, the President shall resume the powers and duties of his office.

---

## AMENDMENT XXVI

*Passed by Congress March 23, 1971. Ratified July 1, 1971.*

**Note**: Amendment 14, section 2, of the Constitution was modified by section 1 of the 26th amendment.

**Section 1.**
The right of citizens of the United States, who are eighteen years of age or older, to vote shall not be denied or abridged by the United States or by any State on account of age.

**Section 2.**
The Congress shall have power to enforce this article by appropriate legislation.

---

## AMENDMENT XXVII

*Originally proposed Sept. 25, 1789. Ratified May 7, 1992.*

No law, varying the compensation for the services of the Senators and Representatives, shall take effect, until an election of Representatives shall have intervened

## States' Rights Under the U.S. Constitution

### Selective incorporation under the 14<sup>th</sup> Amendment

The U.S. Constitution has Articles and Amendments that established constitutional rights.

The provisions in the Bill of Rights (i.e., the first ten Amendments to the Constitution) were initially binding upon only the federal government.

In time, most of these provisions became binding upon the states through *selective incorporation* into the *due process clause* of the 14<sup>th</sup> Amendment (i.e., reverse incorporation).

When a provision is made binding on a state, a state can no longer restrict the rights guaranteed in that provision.

The 1<sup>st</sup> Amendment guarantees the freedoms of speech, press, religion, and assembly.

The 5<sup>th</sup> Amendment protects the right to grand jury proceedings in federal criminal cases

The 6<sup>th</sup> Amendment guarantees a right to confront witnesses (i.e., Confrontation Clause).

The right to confront witnesses was not *selectively incorporated* into the due process clause of the 14<sup>th</sup> Amendment and is not binding upon the states.

Therefore, persons involved in state criminal proceedings as a defendant have no federal constitutional right to grand jury proceedings.

Whether an individual has a right to a grand jury becomes a question of state law.

The 10<sup>th</sup> Amendment, which is part of the Bill of Rights, was ratified on December 15, 1791. It states the Constitution's principle of federalism by providing that powers not granted to the federal government by the Constitution, nor prohibited to the States, are reserved to the States or the people.

### Federalism in the United States

Federalism in the United States is the evolving relationship between state governments and the federal government.

The American government has evolved from a system of dual federalism to associative federalism.

In "Federalist No. 46," James Madison wrote that the states and national government "are in fact but different agents and trustees of the people, constituted with different powers."

Alexander Hamilton, in "Federalist No. 28," suggested that both levels of government would exercise authority to the citizens' benefit: "If their [the peoples'] rights are invaded by either, they can make use of the other as the instrument of redress."[3]

---

Because the states were preexisting political entities, the U.S. Constitution did not need to define or explain federalism in one section, but it often mentions the rights and responsibilities of state governments and state officials in relation to the federal government.

The federal government has certain *express powers* (also called *enumerated powers*), which are powers spelled out in the Constitution, including the right to levy taxes, declare war, and regulate interstate and foreign commerce.

Also, the *Necessary and Proper Clause* gives the federal government the *implied power* to pass any law "necessary and proper" to execute its express powers.

Enumerated powers of the Federal Government are contained in Article I, Section 8 of the U.S. Constitution.

Other powers—the *reserved powers*—are reserved to the people or the states under the 10th Amendment. The Supreme Court decision significantly expanded the power delegated to the federal government in *McCulloch v. Maryland* (1819) and the 13th, 14th and 15th, Amendments to the Constitution following the Civil War.

## *Law Essentials* series

| | |
|---|---|
| Constitutional Law | Criminal Law and Criminal Procedure |
| Contracts | Business Associations |
| Evidence | Conflict of Laws |
| Real Property | Family Law |
| Torts | Secured Transactions |
| Civil Procedure | Trusts and Estates |

**Visit our Amazon store**

### *Comprehensive Glossary of Legal Terms*

Over 2,100 essential legal terms defined and explained. An excellent reference source for law students, practitioners and readers seeking an understanding of legal vocabulary and its application.

### *Landmark U.S. Supreme Court Cases: Essential Summaries*

Learn important constitutional cases that shaped American law. Understand how the evolving needs of society intersect with the U.S. Constitution. Short summaries of seminal Supreme Court cases focused on issues and holdings.

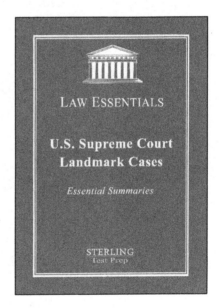

**Visit our Amazon store**

# Frank J. Addivinola, Ph.D., J.D., L.LM., MBA

The lead author and chief editor of this preparation guide is Dr. Frank Addivinola. With his outstanding education, professional training, legal and business experience, and university teaching, Dr. Addivinola lent his expertise to develop this book.

Attorney Frank Addivinola is admitted to practice law in several jurisdictions. He has served as an academic advisor and mentor for students and practitioners.

Dr. Addivinola holds an undergraduate degree from Williams College. He completed his Masters at Harvard University, Masters in Biotechnology at Johns Hopkins University, Masters in Technology Management and MBA at the University of Maryland University College, J.D. and L.LM. from Suffolk University, and Ph.D. in Law and Public Policy from Northeastern University.

During his extensive teaching career, Dr. Addivinola taught university courses in Introduction to Law and developed law coursebooks. He received several awards for community service, research, and presentations.

Made in the USA
Coppell, TX
11 December 2024

42180977R00083